William D. Heffernan

*The
Characteristics
of
Effective
Organizations*

THE CHARACTERISTICS OF EFFECTIVE ORGANIZATIONS

PAUL E. MOTT
University of Pennsylvania

Harper & Row, Publishers
New York, Evanston, San Francisco, London

For my wife, Tish

CONTENTS

PREFACE

The objectives of the research summarized in this book were to define and develop measures of organizational effectiveness and to determine some of the characteristics of organizations that influence their effectiveness. In 1958, when I began this research, virtually all definitions of effectiveness were based on either functionalist principles (like success at achieving goals), simple measures of productivity, or indicator measures (like employee turnover or absenteeism). The inadequacy of these definitions was made clear by Guy E. Swanson, then Professor of Sociology at The University of Michigan, in his lectures on the sociology of large organizations. Those lectures, literally crammed with new ideas and perspectives, excited my own interest in large organizations. After borrowing heavily from Professor Swanson and from an article by Basil Georgopoulos and Arnold Tannenbaum ("A Study of Organizational Effectiveness," American Sociological Review, 22, October 1957: 534–540), I concluded that the concept of effectiveness is multidimensional, involving, besides productivity, the organization's ability to adapt to changing conditions both internal and external (adaptability), and its ability to cope with temporally unpredictable emergencies (flexibility). Using data from a comparative study of hospitals collected and reported by Professor Georgopoulos and Floyd C. Mann, I wrote my doctoral dissertation on the characteristics of hospitals with varying degrees of adaptability and capacities for handling temporally unpredictable emergencies. The results were intriguing because they suggested that the characteristics of organizations that facilitate these distinct facets of effectiveness are often different and sometimes mutually conflicting. Among the many people to whom I am grateful for their help in this project, Professors Georgopoulos, Mann, and Swanson must be named first.

I am also grateful to the Social Science Research Council for a grant that permitted further exploration of the hospital data as well as refinement and extension of the basic findings. These efforts led to the development of a model of effective organizations that I was given an opportunity to test almost immediately in the Office of Administration of the National Aeronautics and Space Administration. Data were collected to test the model; both data and model were used in management seminars that I conducted at NASA. The openness and cooperativeness of the NASA division directors and personnel did much to increase my understanding of how organizations function and to help refine the effectiveness model. Particularly helpful were John D. Young, then head of the Office of Administration, and John Cole and Charles Haynes, who provided the organizational support for my research activities and many insights and ideas that led to further theoretical development and explanation. Rensis Likert, John French, Jr., and Franklin Neff of the Institute for Social Research at The University of Michigan gave generously of their time and thought in coping with problems that arose during this research. All the people mentioned are absolved of responsibility for the views and methods that appear on the pages that follow. Indeed, some of them have argued against views expressed here, though always good-naturedly and with the hope that I might eventually see the light.

Other studies in other organizations followed, and in each, new measures were devised to test hypotheses that had been evolved during previous studies. I am grateful to Daniel Blaine, M.D., Administrator of Philadelphia State Hospital, for the opportunity to collect data there, to the people in "Alpha Agency" who helped me, and to John Croxall, who permitted us to collect data in the Office of Financial Management in the U.S. Department of Health, Education and Welfare.

During these studies I was ably assisted at different times by Anthony Butterfield, Howard Kaplan, and Charles Wheeler. Each has either written a doctoral dissertation from these data or is in the process of doing so. Joan Shadur Pinsky did an excellent job of processing most of the data reported here and also conducted the necessary bibliographical research.

I am greatly indebted to Miss Susan Watson, who gave us much more of her time than we could pay her for to develop our computer programs and to train students to use them. The University of Pennsylvania, in the person of Willis Winn, Dean of the Wharton School, provided vital financial assistance at one critical point so that we could complete our computer programming and data processing.

I am also greatly indebted to my wife for organizing our activities to permit me to concentrate on research, for typing all the many drafts of this book, and for copy editing each draft. The book is as much hers as it is mine and is therefore dedicated to her.

P. E. M.

1
A Preliminary Model of Human Organizations

The characteristics of effective organizations are a topic about which very little is known, despite their importance. Research on the characteristics of effective families is rare; research on other types of organizations is limited to varying degrees.

Before we can discuss the characteristics associated with effectiveness it is necessary to define the concepts that we shall be using, particularly "organization" and "effectiveness." In this chapter we shall outline the elements of a model of organization, essential to understanding the fuller discussion to follow. In Chapter 2 the concept of organizational effectiveness will be defined and appropriate measures explained. Throughout the remainder of the book various organizational characteristics— coordination, leadership styles, methods of communication, and problem solving, structures of decision-making, and so on —will be studied in relation to organizational effectiveness.

TWO POLAR VIEWS OF ORGANIZATIONS

People who work in large organizations or who study them usually elect one of two opposing views. These views can be loosely labeled the "open" and "closed" perspectives. Adherents of the closed perspective tend to set aside or to give inadequate consideration to the effects of the environments in which organizations exist; they concentrate instead on internal workings. The open approach starts with an opposite assumption: As organizations exist in dynamic environments, their functions can be understood best by taking these environments into account. Selection of one of these alternative views makes a critical difference in the type of organizational theory that is developed, and therefore, they must be examined carefully.

The Closed-System Perspective

The personnel specialist who looks at the morale problems of workers only in the context of the factory, without considering possible origins in their home lives; the systems analyst who uses only the materials at hand without taking advantage of new techniques and equipment being used elsewhere; the social scientist who develops his theory of organization after having set aside the effects of the external environment—all these specialists are using a closed-system approach to the organizations that they work in or study. They tend to discount or to underemphasize the role of the environment in the affairs of the organization. They seldom actually deny the importance of environment in organizational activity; rather, they simply set it aside to concentrate on internal problems and functions.

Theories arising from this approach have a mechanical character. Management is said to specify clear goals; then, through a process of rationalization, the activities necessary to achieve those goals are determined and assigned to roles to be performed by people. Such theories alone are not enough to produce a closed-system model; the latter results from a formal and highly structured approach that specifies in precise detail the activities associated with roles and relationships among roles. A football play or an assembly-line operation is an example of a situation in which those in the various roles have been told precisely what to do and how their tasks relate to those of others around them. Because of their mechanical character, such models are usually labeled "structuralist" though not all structuralist models are also closed-system models. Most reflect implicit, and sometimes explicit, emphasis on designing organizations to maximize efficient routine production: The structures that they create are intended to facilitate it.

Such models have much to commend them. The concept of role is certainly very useful in social theories, and its parallel in business organizations, the job description, has considerable practical utility. Related notions of formal coordination, communications networks, and delegated authority also have both theoretical and practical uses.

The Open-System Perspective

Adherents of the open-system approach consider the environment as the major reality with which any organization must cope. Organizations exist in constantly changing environments and must adjust to them. Any given organizational structure, then, should be temporary: Flux, rather than rigid structure, should characterize the internal workings of the organization. Ad hoc groups are formed and dissolved as old problems are solved and new ones arise. Changes in roles and shifts in relations with others are frequent and desirable. Usually authority is shared equally among the members of groups, rather than being parceled unequally among different roles: The hierarchy is flattened out.

In addition to emphasizing organizational adaptability, rather than productivity, an antistructural value is usually either explicit or implicit in these theories, for two reasons. First, it seems difficult, perhaps impossible, to design rigid roles and role relations adequate to deal with the often unpredictable stimuli that come from changing environments. Greater reliance must be placed on individuals who can improvise as necessary to adjust to new problems and opportunities. These individuals should therefore not be tightly constrained by roles. Second, many adherents of open-system approaches themselves attach great value to human fulfillment, or "self-actualization," in work and to the fullest possible use of individual creativity in solving organizational problems. Many of them believe that structured organizations minimize achievement of these objectives. They prefer to scrap such concepts as control and coordination, roles and job descriptions, and graded authority and to replace them with notions of self-actualization, self-esteem, group problem-solving, and pooled or shared authority.

The open-system perspective also can make valuable contributions to the theory and practice of large organizations. Environments do exist and do have profound effects on the organizations in them; organizations themselves are composed of people whose own needs are related in the most fundamental ways to how they do their work. Concepts like self-esteem and adaptability have great utility in the study of large organizations.

Some Problems Arising from Closed- and Open-System Approaches

Closed-system formulations suffer from certain assumptions (or lack of them) about the environment and the human beings that work in organizations—the occupants of those neatly articulated roles. Environments do pose problems for organizations, problems to which they must often adjust if they are to remain viable. Some owners of smoothly operating, efficient firms that manufactured silk stockings were suddenly out of business because they had failed to adopt the new synthetic fabrics that had been developed outside their organizations. Adaptability is more difficult for highly structured organizations than for less structured ones (though they can ease the difficulties somewhat by developing special units responsible for scanning the environment for potentially relevant problems). This inability to adapt results because people trained to operate in certain roles and to relate to others in specified ways have difficulty behaving differently. Football coaches with highly "programmed" teams often complain that the teams have difficulty in adjusting to opponents who behave unexpectedly in ways for which the teams are not programmed. Nor is adaptability to new situations one of the virtues of an automated assembly line.

On the other hand, employees themselves sometimes recognize the dynamic character of their environment and exhibit a disarming willingness to improvise in new situations. In such instances job descriptions become virtually meaningless, and annual plans are relegated to the remotest parts of workers' desks. The organization loses its neatness, roles are improvised, and informal horizontal communication about work problems becomes commonplace.

Even if the environment presented few problems, however, people in closed-system organizations would create problems in their work. The demands of their jobs often stifle their creativity or do not match their interests or abilities. Very often they can think of other ways to do their jobs or of other things that they would like to do, but, because following suggestions would disrupt routine productivity, the suggestions are often rejected. Advocates of highly structured organizations do want some innovative people, but they want even these people to calculate the benefits of each innovation against its costs in disrupting productivity and to learn to make their innovations with a minimum disturbance to the existing structure.

The responses of closed-system theorists to such problems have been varied. Some try to increase their organizational adaptability by designing structures in which people are obliged to make disciplined responses to "political" executives who bring to the organizations or are sensitive to the problems and demands of the social environment. Others have adopted a scientific-management approach, trying to fit the man to the job and thus, they hope, evading problems caused by human personality. Others add to job descriptions that ubiquitous escape clause: "and other duties as assigned." Still others, found mainly among academic theorists, have invented a kind of organizational schizophrenia: the formal and informal systems within one organization. The formal system is the closed one in which productivity is emphasized, whereas the informal system emphasizes coping with the unusual and finding ways to deal with the inadequacies of the formal system. Wherever it has been accepted this last formulation has given rise to a new problem and a new activity: adapting the informal system to meet the needs of the formal one.

Open-system approaches suffer from a reverse set of problems. They usually give inadequate attention to the importance of productivity and the utility of structures designed to achieve it. It is probably not accidental that much of the research on and application of open-system approaches is directed toward scientific and other innovative kinds of organization or to the most innovative parts of productive organizations.

As there is much that is theoretically and practically useful in both the open and closed views, it is important to achieve some synthesis of them.

DEVELOPING ANOTHER VIEW OF ORGANIZATION

The dilemma of open versus closed theories of organization cannot be resolved simply by amalgamating them because the assumptions and values implicit in them are often contradictory. Most closed-system theorists assume that the organization maintains natural boundaries whereas open-system theorists treat the organization as more intimately related to its environments. The former usually value balance, stability, order, and quantitative growth, whereas the latter value autonomy, change, action, and qualitative growth in the self-esteem of the members. This list of contradictory assumptions and values could be lengthened considerably, but the point is clear: Trying to amalgamate them is as integrative as juxtaposing the halves of an apple and an orange.

James D. Thompson has proposed a different solution, one that focuses on the hierarchical character of large organizations.[1] At the lower levels of organization—the technical core, where the work is highly rationalized and routinized —the closed-system view is most appropriate. But at the upper levels of organization such routine cannot be achieved, and an open-system approach is desirable. The middle level—the managerial level—links the two. This hierarchical solution is unacceptable, however, because it is based on unrealistic organizational stereotypes. It is easy to make a case for the reverse proposition that the open system is more apparent in the technical core. Many people at this level (for example, the social worker, the mailman, the auditor, and the personnel specialist) are in closer contact with the social environment and are more directly affected by it than are the institutional leaders. In fact, one major complaint from personnel at this level is that they are hampered unnecessarily by remote leaders whose directives reflect no understanding of what the real world is like. But this proposition is also unrealistic, for, in fact, open-system properties are found at every level in the organization, though they may vary in type and intensity with location. Institutional leaders are in contact with and influenced by the social environment but probably by different aspects of the social environment from those that influence lower-level workers. Closed-system properties are also found at every level. Perhaps they are somewhat more common at the technical core than at the managerial level, but they are present everywhere.

Our position is that no formulation amalgamating or allocating the elements of open- and closed-system theories in their present forms can resolve the theoretical difficulties outlined. The assumptions and concepts on which these theories are based must themselves be modified. Certain criteria for the necessary modifications of existing views appeal to us. First, a serviceable theory of human organization should be based on the assumption that no human organization is completely closed to its environment but that nevertheless *there is always some degree of closure, which varies from one or-*

[1] James D. Thompson, *Organizations in Action* (New York: McGraw-Hill, 1967).

ganization to another. Second, as the structuring of roles and groups and the relationships among them is the major method of achieving organizational closure, it follows that these roles and relationships must also be considered as varying in degree of closure and thus in clarity and predictability. Theoretical allowances must be made for varying degrees of improvisation within and among roles, including improvisations that conflict with the definitions of those roles and the associated relationships. A less simplistic conception of relationship than is usually found in closed-system theories is also necessary. We turn now to more detailed considerations of these assumptions.

Closure as a Variable Concept

It is observable that organizations vary in degree of closure. Some public bureaucracies are more resistant than are others to the importunings of clients, legislators, chief executives, and lobbyists. Some villages are more insulated from change originating in the larger society than are others.

The members of most organizations usually try to achieve some closure for their organizations: to reduce the *variety* of inputs. Young people "go steady" or marry, rather than "playing the field"; work units that will produce standardized products are created; and potential markets are the objects of massive campaigns of persuasion designed to stimulate desire for the standard products of the producing organization. Without some closure organizational life would be very difficult. The members would be aware of, and would often react to, a bewildering array of stimuli that would prevent them from spending time doing what they wanted or ought to do. The individual might feel insecure and not in control of his own organizational future; most human beings prefer reasonable measures of security and control in their lives. The advantages of partial system closure are well known and well documented, as in the example of the village gatekeeper whose role preserves the existing values and power configurations of the village by controlling the exposure of villagers to outsiders and outside influences; or the restaurant cook who learns to control the inputs from waitresses to preserve his own status and to control his own circumstances.[2] The danger lies in going too far and eliminating apparently extraneous but actually meaningful

[2] William F. Whyte, *Human Relations in the Restaurant Industry* (New York: McGraw-Hill, 1948).

stimuli from the environment. The open-closed property of organizations is thus continuous, rather than discrete. Organizations vary in their openness, but most are probably nearer to the open end than to the closed end of the continuum.

Closure can be obtained by structuring input and output processes. Practically this end is obtained by structuring organizational roles and groups, particularly those in contact with the environment, as well as the relationships among them. People are assigned roles or tasks that are highly structured (the closed organizational component), specific sets of activities that leave no room for improvisation. When roles and groups, particularly those in closest contact with the environment, are highly structured, extraneous stimuli from the environment are more likely to go unnoticed or to be rejected. There are obvious dangers, as well as benefits, in this method of obtaining closure. Normal production may proceed efficiently, but, when the unusual occurs, workers may react inadequately, slowly, or not at all. A few of the hospitals from which the data in the following chapters were gathered were very successful in structuring the routine tasks of the nursing staff; these same hospitals, however, had difficulty in handling emergencies because the performances required were not in the workers' job descriptions. Other organizations have experienced difficulties precisely *because* certain tasks have been included in job descriptions. The Texas state police, for example, found that too often policemen delayed the handling of emergencies by insisting on assuming leadership in the ad hoc groups already coping with emergencies, thus interfering with the activities of these groups. The police were then instructed to assist rescue efforts already underway, rather than reorganize them.

Some tasks are relatively unstructured (the open organizational component). They usually occur when people must be aware of and react to wide ranges of environmental stimuli, when the activities constituting the tasks are quite complex or include some demand for improvisation, and when it is not clear precisely what objectives should be pursued (as in scientific research).

On the basis of our discussion we believe that the degree of organizational closure affects the applicability of various theoretical concepts. Concepts like role (and status) are increasingly useful predictors as closure increases. Talcott Parsons' emphasis on the "status-role bundle" in *The Social System* has maximum theoretical utility as long as his assumptions about closure (which permitted him to focus on the internal processes of social change but do not necessarily reflect belief on his part that systems are actually closed) are accepted.[3] But, as organizational openness increases, the theoretical utility of the concept of role decreases, and that of the more social-psychological concept of "person" increases. For example, we shall show later that in coping with a hospital emergency (an open-system condition) dimensions of person vie with dimensions of role as predictors of success. An open organization requires considerable improvisation among its members; they give each other information about what tasks need to be done and who should do them (role-sending and role-taking). Personal traits like intelligence, experience, courage, and commitment to the organization are essential to successful improvisation.

But recognition of closure as a variable and of the differences in the utility of various concepts as closure varies does not resolve the problem of how to establish a single conceptual framework that can be used regardless of degree of closure. In order to establish such a framework, we must begin by recognizing that there are forces in organizations operating toward structuring of roles and role relationships and others operating toward increasing the scope for improvisation in roles and associated relationships.

In every organization there are people engaged in control and coordination, in creating, modifying, and destroying structures. Basically they set parameters for acceptable human activity by prescribing tasks and intertask relationships. Sometimes they are too zealous and at other times perhaps not zealous enough in their efforts to specify formal procedures for every contingency; they cannot structure responses for all situations, however. Within the imposed parameters it remains for workers to solve the unanticipated but often important problems that arise by informally negotiating new activities and relations among themselves. (Anselm Strauss and his colleagues have called these relations *negotiated or-*

---

[3] Talcott Parsons, *The Social System* (New York: Free Press, 1951).

ders.[4]) This statement is rather conservative, and we add quickly that the people who negotiate orders can also attempt to alter the control parameters themselves. The two (parameters and negotiated orders) are in shifting equilibriums, depending upon the organization. In some organizations management attempts to stifle the development of negotiated orders by specifying detailed procedures; in others the parameters are few, and negotiating orders is the dominant method of solving problems. Both setting parameters and negotiating orders should occur, and the ratio of their prevalence in an effective organization is a function of two dimensions mentioned earlier: amenability of tasks to structuring and vulnerability of task structure to the environment.

For example, in some colleges and universities, like the U.S. Military Academy, fairly detailed and restrictive parameters for student activities have been set by the staffs. The hours of going to bed and rising, permissible types and places of social activity, and modes of interaction with others are all prescribed. In other universities only a few such parameters exist. Female students are required to be in their residences by certain hours at night, and students are required to wear certain types of clothing. In still others all such regulations have been eliminated, often under pressure from the students themselves. The areas in which students are free to improvise solutions to problems — to negotiate their own orders with others — thus vary in scope.

What is a negotiated order? It is a pattern of relationships among people improvised, either individually or collectively, by them in response to problems. For collective solutions people must be able to meet easily to exchange ideas and propose solutions. People solve some problems of coordination simply by *not* creating problems for one another or by staying out of one another's way. These solutions may become fairly permanent, or they may be quite ephemeral, but either way they can help the organization to function more effectively.

In summary, we can say that two vital processes occur in large organizations: formal coordination and informal, moment-by-moment improvisation of solutions to problems.

[4] Anselm Strauss *et al.*, "The Hospital and Its Negotiated Order," in *The Hospital in Modern Society*, ed. Eliot Freidson (New York: Free Press, 1963), pp. 147-169.

These activities can overlap, in the sense that they can be addressed to the same problems, but generally, as closure of the organization increases, the array of problems solved by informal negotiation decreases. This reduction may be either an intentional or an unintentional consequence of formal coordination and the development of custom. Leaders must, however, be aware of this consequence of their organization-building activities, for otherwise they may impair the adaptability of their organizations and stifle the individuality and creativity of the members.

Formal and informal, closed and open aspects of organization are thus integrated into a single construct. The research question then becomes: What are the criteria for determining the optimal combination of formal and informal problem solving for different organizations at different times, in order to optimize productivity and adaptability? Or in order to maximize both individual self-actualization and organizational effectiveness? These critical questions are among those to be examined in the ensuing chapters. But before we can discuss them it is necessary to complete our survey of the basic concepts that we shall use in treating organizational closure as a variable. Having outlined the concepts of role, parameter setting, negotiated orders, and role taking and sending, we turn now to relationships among roles and among groups.

Relationships Among Roles and Groups

Because it seems useful to conceptualize roles and groups as centers of power and authority, we shall first discuss the concepts of social power and authority. Few notions are of greater importance in the study of social organization than is that of social power, yet there is little agreement on how to define and measure it. Some social scientists define it as a kind of action, whereas others view it as a *potential* for action. Elements of force and coercion are central to some definitions but absent from others. In still others power is presented as an intrinsic organizational property, and there are those who locate it specifically in the decision-making structure. We have reviewed these definitions elsewhere,[5] with an eye to theoretical

[5] Paul E. Mott, "Power, Influence, and Authority," in *The Structure of Community Power*, ed. Michael Aiken and Mott (New York: Random House, 1970), pp. 3-16.

and practical use, and have arrived at the following working definition: *Social power is the usable and socially valued latent energy in human organizations.*

Human organizations are energy-binding systems: The very act of ordering human behavior binds the energies of individuals, by making some of these energies available for collective activities.[6] The sum of the individual energies available for collective activities represents much of the total social power of a group. Other socially valued resources such as money are also sources of social power because possession enables some control over the energies of others. Access to this latent energy, derived from human beings and from the control of resources, is ordinarily obtained by assuming roles in the organization. Different roles give access to different amounts of social power. Individuals are said to be more or less powerful, depending upon the amount of power to which their roles give them access, particularly when they use that power to order the behavior of others. That is, social power is not self-directed energy; agents direct it in a variety of ways, coercive or otherwise. The behavior of people is ordered directly by the powerful or indirectly through their own needs to adjust to centers of power in order to maximize their own life chances. Human groups are thus energy-binding systems and can be regarded as centers of power related to other centers of power in an organization.

Social influence is the attempt to use the energies of others to achieve desired objectives. Whereas social power is latent, influence is kinetic. It consists of activity: suppressing, refusing, directing, persuading, and so forth. It is also purely social, occurring only in the various forms of human interaction. It is related to social power in that those who occupy roles that have high access to power are more likely to be successful in their attempts to influence than are those who do not.

Social authority is also related to social power in that it involves either legitimizing existing centers of power (such as the coronation of Napoleon) or authorizing new centers of legitimate power. The National Aeronautics and Space Administration (NASA) and the U.S. State Department were created

[6] Leslie A. White, *The Science of Culture* (New York; Grove Press, 1949); and Amos H. Hawley, "Community Power and Urban Renewal Success," *The American Journal of Sociology* 68 (1963): 422-431.

by legitimate means. The right to use certain resources to a-chieve selected objectives was assigned, and within each organization a series of offices was created, each with some authority. Similar statements can be made about the hospitals studied here, though the processes of authorization differed in some details.

Viewed in this perspective, large organizations are collections of centers of power (and authority), in which the degree of centralization of power varies considerably; that is, in which the relations among the centers of power can vary from highly integrated to highly diffuse. The dimension of centralization-decentralization of power and authority will be discussed in Chapter 4, but the degree of integration of relations among the centers of power requires immediate attention.

Any conceptual scheme in which closure is a variable must, for reasons that we have already discussed, be based on a more general notion of relations than is found in closed-system formulations. For this purpose we have adopted the engineering concept of interface—used to describe relations among different machine systems or between machine and human systems—to describe the relations among groups and roles. Interfaces can take many forms, but there are two major dimensions along which these forms vary: degree of structure and directness of connection. To say that an interface is structured is to say that common norms for communication and exchange activities exist and are followed by people in institutionalized roles. When interfaces are not organized relations are ephemeral and often improvised, there are few common norms, and there is an abundance of role-sending and role-taking activity. Direct relations are those in which the centers of power interact without intermediaries. Indirect relations involve intermediaries. Parties to litigation have indirect interfaces because they use lawyers as intermediaries. The need to send messages through three or more levels of a hierarchy reveals indirect interfaces. Table 1-1 summarizes these types of relations.

This categorization could be further generalized by adding a dimension of specificity-diffuseness, but the two dimensions in Table 1-1 are most relevant to the types of organizations to be studied here. Labor-management negotiations to-

TABLE 1-1 Types of Interfaces in Large Organizations

	DIRECTLY CONNECTED	INDIRECTLY CONNECTED	NOT CONNECTED
Organized	Direct exchanges between centers of power employing institutional role-status systems and guided by common norms	Institutionalized use of third parties or a special exchange culture as means of interaction between centers of power	The centers of power are segmented by mutual agreement
Unorganized	Direct exchanges between centers of power involving considerable improvisation, ephemeral or nonexistent role statuses and norms, and ad hoc relations	Intentional or unintentional effects of the centers of power on one another through intermediaries	Circumstantial lack of connection between centers of power

day are usually organized and direct, though in earlier stages of their development they were more unorganized though direct. When these negotiations reach an impasse or break down, the parties often resort to the organized indirect interface. The famous silent trading systems of some South Pacific islands offer an interesting example of an organized indirect interface, in which the intermediary is a very elaborate system of shared norms of exchange, rather than a third party. Unorganized indirect interfaces involve simple chain reactions of influence. For instance, the activities of power center A cause adjustment in B, which causes additional responses in C. A company doubles its work force, causing real-estate developers to build new homes, the city to build new streets and sewers, and the school board to plan new elementary schools. Dissolution of a friendship or a marriage can result in an organized, unconnected interface: The individuals or groups involved agree not to communicate in the future. Unorganized and unconnected centers of power simply have no exchanges, whether or not the lack is desirable. Historically many associations of blacks have had this type of interface with some white centers of power.

The concept of interface is theoretically very useful. It opens our thinking to the great variety of relations that can exist among groups and raises a number of provocative questions. How are the different types of interfaces related to the effectiveness of the groups involved? Is this relationship a functional one, depending upon situational factors? What happens when groups present different types of organization at their interfaces—as when one is highly organized and the other is not? Are there patterns in the natural histories of interfaces between groups? Do they tend to become institutionalized over time? What types of interfaces are associated with the greatest understanding by each group of the needs, problems, and points of view of the other? With effective problem-solving? With intergroup tension, violence, and conflict?

CONCLUSIONS

In this chapter we have been developing a more general model of large organizations than is usually found in the literature on so-called "formal" organizations. Here large organizations are conceptualized as collections of centers of power in varying degrees of centralization, related to one another through interfaces that vary in degree of organization and directness of connection. Internal structure is constantly being created and destroyed by the twin functions of formal coordination and informal negotiation. Organizations are thus in permanent flux, but the amount of this flux varies from one organization to another. As roles and relationships become increasingly structured, the organization becomes more and more impervious to its environment—unless it develops special units with the specific function of scanning the environment and informing organizational leaders of their findings.

Among the advantages of this model is an opportunity to study the conditions that lead to varying degrees of closure in different organizations. Another is that so-called "formal" organizations can be linked theoretically more closely with models of other social organizations like communities, associations, and society itself. It is probably true that "formal" organizations may have proportionally more organized direct interfaces than do communities, associations, and societies, but the difference is one of degree, rather than of kind. Finally, Max Weber's ideal bureaucracy and similar constructs can be treated as examples nearer the closed end of the organizational continuum, rather than as modal, or even desirable, structures for large organizations.[7]

[7] Max Weber, *The Theory of Social and Economic Organization*, 2nd ed., trans. A. M. Henderson and Talcott Parsons (New York: Free Press, 1947), pp. 329-341.

In conclusion, we believe that *the degree of organizational closure is an important variable mediating many of the relationships between other organizational properties and organizational effectiveness.* The ways in which many organizational characteristics are related to organizational effectiveness are thus determined by the degree of structuring of roles or tasks and of relationships among roles and groups. Our research program called for the development of measures of the structuring of roles or tasks (development of similar measures of the characteristics of interfaces was deferred to future research projects because they are very complex and require considerable questionnaire space). Measuring task structuring proved very difficult. We used four different methods (in three studies we were looking for a shorter questionnaire method than that of F. Fiedler, which we had used at one site), but only one had sufficient validity to permit reporting results. We therefore have data on task structuring from only two of our research sites.

In the next chapter we shall discuss and define the concept of organizational effectiveness and describe measures for it. A description of the sites at which our data were gathered will also be presented there. The remainder of the book will be devoted to discussion of relationships between selected organizational characteristics and organizational effectiveness. In Chapter 3 various measures of organizational integration will be examined in relation to effectiveness. In Chapter 4 we shall examine the relative effectiveness of different styles of decision-making in large organizations. In Chapter 5 the relationships between the needs of individuals and effectiveness will be discussed. In the remaining two chapters, one written by a former graduate student who worked with the author, we shall review and discuss what has probably been the most common concern among students of large organizations: What styles of leadership are related to effective group functioning?

2
Defining and
Measuring Organizational
Effectiveness

We define organizational effectiveness as *the ability of an organization to mobilize its centers of power for action—production and adaptation.* Effective organizations are those that produce more and higher-quality outputs and adapt more effectively to environmental and internal problems than do other, similar organizations. But production and adaptation are themselves very complex processes and must be examined more closely.

There are several important criteria for organizing centers of power for routine production. The quantity and quality of the product are important for the relative survival capabilities of an organization. Efficiency—achievement of the greatest output for the least input—is a third criterion that influences the relative well-being of an organization. All three of these criteria weigh in very complex equations involving resource-product exchanges with other organizations. Because of situational differences the weight assigned to each criterion varies from one organization to another. But the key theoretical question is: How should the centers of power be organized to achieve each of these three production objectives? Are the appropriate organizational styles the same or different for each objective?

The necessity for organizing centers of power to change or add routines derives partly from organizations' existence in dynamic environments that are constantly posing new problems and solutions to existing problems. Organizations that adapt to their environments are more effective in the long run than are those that do not. An oil refinery that adopts computer technology is more likely to survive than is one that continues to rely on a large labor force. The rare school system that has adjusted its teaching techniques to meet the needs and problems of the culturally disadvantaged among its students is certainly more effective than are the majority of systems that have not.

Problems also originate inside the organization. No organization ever fulfills the needs of all its members, nor is it ever completely free of conflict. Communities have exhibited varying degrees of willingness to deal with the problems of the poor in their midst. Corporation managers have demonstrated varying abilities and degrees of willingness to deal with their firms' internal problems. And, even when these managers have shown inventiveness and adaptive capacity, those whom they lead have not always been willing to change. This writer was interviewing the chief of the nursing staff in a hospital when the storeroom supervisor interrupted. He asked what she wanted done with some cases of disposable syringes that were gathering dust in the storeroom. Because this type of syringe saves considerable time and money, in comparison with that involved in using the glass syringes, the administrator had purchased them without consulting the chief of nursing. She replied to the storeroom supervisor, "Well, I guess they appeared by magic, and I assume they will disappear the same way." A useful innovation was avoided because of a complex set of internal problems.

Like organizing for production, adaptability is a multifaceted process. It has two major phases: symbolic and behavioral adaptation. Symbolic adaptation begins when members of organizations become aware of problems.[1] People are relatively adaptive if they become aware of problems before they seriously affect the organization. But such awareness does not always develop. Most Americans were not aware of the prevalence and severity of poverty in this country before a combination of books, articles, and television programs brought it to their attention. Unfortunately millions of people and many generations had suffered the effects of poverty before any significant mobilization of resources to cope with it occured. Are some organizational structures more conducive than others to early awareness of problems? We hear of execu-

---

[1] W. J. Gore, "Decision Making in Federal Field Offices," *Public Administration Review* 16 (1956): 281-290.

tives who have no time for advance planning and of those who do. We know of families that plan for future problems and those that give no thought to what the end of the day may bring. How do we explain these differences?

Second, even when the necessary awareness exists, little is gained unless appropriate solutions are formulated. This step requires a combination of knowledge of the tools and techniques that can be used to solve the problem and correct decisions on how to use them. Again there are abundant illustrations of organizations whose members know about problems but are immobilized by the prospect of solving them and of others whose members solve problems promptly and well. The probability of finding the most adequate solution is also a function of the range of proposed solutions and of the ability to choose among them rapidly and well. Are some organizational structures more conducive than are others to large numbers and broad ranges of possible solutions and to judicious selection among them? The findings from telephone experiments by Alex Bavelas clearly show that, given similar information but different decision-making structures, certain types of structures will facilitate problem-solving more than others will.[2]

Third, even when useful solutions are generated, they are still symbols, not behavior. Symbolic exercise is little more than exercise unless appropriate behavioral adaptation follows. We propose two behavioral criteria of adaptability: the proportion of relevant members who accept the changes and the rapidity with which they accept them. Performance according to these criteria undoubtedly also varies from one organization to another. What organizational characteristics are associated with these variations?

There is one special type of adaptive problem that we shall separate from the general category just discussed: organizational ability to adjust its centers of power quickly to cope with temporally unpredictable overloads of work that require significant but temporary modifications of roles by affected members. This special form of adaptability we shall call "organizational flexibility." Communities suffer natural and man-made disasters. Hospitals are confronted with sudden, unpre-

[2]Alex Bavelas, "Communication Patterns in Task-Oriented Groups," *Journal of the Acoustical Society of America* 22 (1950): 725-730.

dictable case loads because of multiple automobile accidents, fires, and other disasters. Government agencies receive from the President orders to set up major programs in short periods of time. The organization of effort to cope with such situations is different from that for a predictable work overload. The management of a department store knows that it is going to experience a great increase in business volume before Christmas and can plan accordingly. University registration would be drastically different if universities had no idea when students would arrive to register. But who can predict when a fire will occur, when an enemy will attack, when a ship will blow up in the harbor? Flexibility is conceptually different from adaptability because the organizational changes that result from meeting emergencies are usually temporary; usually the organization returns to its pre-emergency structure. Adaptive changes are likely to be more permanent.

Our criteria of effectiveness are summarized in this outline.

A. Organizing centers of power for routine production (productivity)
   1. The quantity of the product
   2. The quality of the product
   3. The efficiency with which it is produced

B. Organizing centers of power to change routines (adaptability)
   1. Symbolic adaptation
      a. anticipating problems in advance and developing satisfactory and timely solutions to them
      b. staying abreast of new technologies and methods applicable to the activities of the organization
   2. Behavioral adaptation
      a. prompt acceptance of solutions
      b. prevalent acceptance of solutions

C. Organizing centers of power to cope with temporally unpredictable overloads of work (flexibility)

MEASURING ORGANIZATIONAL EFFECTIVENESS

The ideal measure of effectiveness would be both valid and reliable, as well as easy and inexpensive to obtain. The latter two criteria have led many researchers to use productivity data collected from or by the organization being studied, but such data have invariably had serious flaws. First, although measures of productivity can reflect the past effectiveness of an organization in adapting to problems and coping with emergencies, they tell us nothing about its viability now or in the future. Second, raw productivity measures exclude considerations of quality and production efficiency. Even unit-cost measures are inadequate because an organization with lower unit costs may actually be devoting inadequate resources to activities that might enhance future effectiveness. Measures of turnover and absenteeism are inadequate as measures of effectiveness; at best, they are indicators. For these reasons we have elected to follow the promising lead of Basil S. Georgopoulos and Floyd C. Mann[3] in attempting to construct a valid subjective measure of organizational effectiveness.

In this section we shall describe our methods of constructing subjective measures of effectiveness. Our studies of the validity of these measures were reassuring. The subjective assessments of work units by the individuals who participated in them were supported by the assessments of top managers responsible for all the units studied in a particular organization and of people in other units whose work made them familiar with that of the units being assessed. The least valid responses were obtained from units whose workers were using outmoded professional criteria to judge the effectiveness of their own work groups. But this problem could be located by comparing the self-evaluations of each work group with those made by people outside who were familiar with the unit's work, and then investigating the causes of large differences between them. Problems also arose when the work of the unit studied was secret, for then the evaluations of outsiders tended to be less reliable. A detailed discussion of our findings on the validity of these measures can be found in Appendix A.

The questionnaire items used to measure effectiveness follow.

Every worker produces something in his work. It may be a "product" or a "service." But sometimes it is very difficult to identify the product or service. Below are listed some of

[3] Basil S. Georgopoulos and Floyd C. Mann, *The Community General Hospital* (New York: Macmillan, 1962).

the products and services being produced in the Office of Administration.[4]

Typed pages	Recommended policies and
Delivered mail	procedures
Dispatched automobiles	New programs
Staff papers and studies	Classified jobs
Coding systems	Supplying new equipment
	Contracts

These are just a few of the things being produced.

We would like you to think carefully of the things that you produce in your work and of the things produced by those people who work around you in your division.

(Production: Quantity)
  Thinking now of the various things produced by the people you know *in your division*, how much are they producing?

  _____(1) Their production is very low
  _____(2) It is fairly low
  _____ (3) It is neither high nor low
  _____ (4) It is fairly high
  _____(5) It is very high

(Production: Quality)
  How good would you say is the *quality* of the products or services produced by the people you know *in your division*?

  _____(1) Their products or services are of poor
                      quality
  _____(2) Their quality is not too good
  _____(3) Fair quality
  _____(4) Good quality
  _____(5) Excellent quality

(Production: Efficiency)
  Do the people in your division seem to get maximum output from the resources (money, people, equipment, etc.) they have available? That is, how *efficiently* do they do their work?

4 The names of other agencies studied were substituted when appropriate.

_____(1) They do not work efficiently at all
_____(2) Not too efficient
_____(3) Fairly efficient
_____(4) They are very efficient
_____(5) They are extremely efficient

(Adaptation: Anticipating Problems and Solving Them Satisfactorily)

How good a job is done by the people in your division
in *anticipating* problems that may come up in the future
and preventing them from occurring or minimizing their
effects?

_____(1) They do a poor job in anticipating
problems
_____(2) Not too good a job
_____(3) A fair job
_____(4) They do a very good job
_____(5) They do an excellent job in anticipat-
ing problems

(Adaptation: Awareness of Potential Solutions)

From time to time newer ways are discovered to organize
work, and newer equipment and techniques are found
with which to do the work. How good a job do the people in your division do at keeping up with those changes
that could affect the way they do their work?

_____(1) They do a poor job of keeping up to
date
_____(2) Not too good a job
_____(3) A fair job
_____(4) They do a good job
_____(5) They do an excellent job of keeping
up to date

(Adaptation: Promptness of Adjustment)

When changes are made in the routines or equipment,
how *quickly* do the people in your division accept and
adjust to these changes?

_____(1) Most people accept and adjust to
them very slowly
_____(2) Rather slowly

_____(3) Fairly rapidly

_____(4) They adjust very rapidly, but not
immediately

_____(5) Most people accept and adjust to
them immediately

(Adaptation: Prevalence of Adjustment)

What *proportion* of the people in your division readily
accept and adjust to these changes?

_____(1) Considerably less than half of the
people accept and adjust to these
changes readily

_____(2) Slightly less than half do

_____(3) The majority do

_____(4) Considerably more than half do

_____(5) Practically everyone accepts and
adjusts to these changes readily

(Flexibility)

From time to time emergencies arise, such as crash programs, schedules moved ahead, or a breakdown in the
flow of work occurs. When these emergencies occur, they
cause work overloads for many people. Some work groups
cope with these emergencies more readily and successfully than others. How good a job do the people in your
division do at coping with these situations?

_____(1) They do a poor job of handling
emergency situations

_____(2) They do not do very well

_____(3) They do a fair job

_____(4) They do a good job

_____(5) They do an excellent job of handling
these situations

These items, along with others used to assess other organizational properties, were included in every questionnaire
administered at the research sites. In constructing the index of
effectiveness for productivity, we scored each respondent's
answers to the three items according to the numbers next to
the options that he selected. These numbers were added, and
the sum divided by three to give a productivity score ranging
between 1.00 and 5.00. When a respondent did not answer

one or more of the component items, no index score was constructed for him (this same procedure was applied to every index in the study). In constructing a score for a given organizational division the mean productivity scores for each person in that division were added; the total was then divided by the number of respondents in that division. The adaptability index was constructed by the same method, using the four adaptation items on the questionnaire.

An overall effectiveness score was obtained for each respondent by totaling his responses to all eight items and then dividing the sum by eight to obtain a mean score between 1.00 and 5.00. A division effectiveness score was obtained by totaling individual effectiveness scores of all respondents from the division and dividing the sum by the total number of respondents from that division. The result was a division score ranging between 1.00 and 5.00. No attempt was made to assign artificial weights to the components of this index of overall effectiveness. Instead, we relied on all four indexes. As a result of this approach the overall measure of effectiveness emphasizes productivity and adaptability, rather than flexibility.

Table 2-1 shows the product-moment correlations among these indexes and between the indexes and their component items for the first study at the National Aeronautics and Space Administration (NASA). The correlations among the three indexes of effectiveness are all positive, statistically significant, but moderate in size. None explains more than 25 percent of the variance in the others. They are not, therefore, mere reproductions of one another. They appear to measure three different, but related, organizational processes, which lends support to our belief in the value of the index of overall effectiveness. Tables for the other studies can be found in Appendix B; they reveal the same basic patterns found in Table 2-2.

DESCRIPTIONS OF THE RESEARCH SETTINGS

Our research strategy can be summed up in the expression "opportunistic comparative organizational studies." Sites where effectiveness could be studied were added as their availability became known to us. Our initial data came from Georgopoulos and Mann's study of ten community general hospitals. These hospitals were randomly selected from all medium-sized, short-stay hospitals in Michigan cities of more than 10,000 people.

TABLE 2-1 Correlations of Effectiveness Items, NASA-1

| | PRODUC-TIVITY | ADAPT-ABILITY | FLEXI-BILITY | PRODUCTIVITY | | | ADAPTABILITY | | | |
				QUAN-TITY	QUAL-ITY	EFFI-CIENCY	ANTICI-PATING PROBLEMS	KEEPING UP TO DATE	PROMPT-NESS OF ADJUST-MENT	PREVA-LENCE OF ADJUST-MENT
Overall effectiveness	.66*	.85	.64	.53	.53	.59	.70	.70	.66	.69
Productivity		.51	.41	.85	.79	.86	.41	.44	.37	.38
Adaptability			.48	.37	.43	.47	.73	.72	.83	.79
Flexibility				.32	.36	.36	.45	.44	.28	.27
Productivity										
Quantity					.49	.61	.29	.27	.29	.29
Quality						.56	.34	.41	.30	.32
Efficiency							.41	.46	.34	.33
Adaptability										
Anticipating problems								.51	.41	.35
Keeping up to date									.39	.32
Promptness of adjustment										.68
Prevalence of adjustment										

*Pearson product-moment correlation coefficients. A missing-data program was used. N = 400–438; $p(.05)$ = .10; $p(.01)$ = .18. Correlations between index items and the indexes of which they are parts are indicated by boxes.

About 1200 questionnaires and interviews were completed, an average of 120 per hospital. [5] The author worked as a research assistant on this project and analyzed the data on the characteristics of hospitals associated with behavioral adaptability and flexibility. [6] The results suggested, first, the potential usefulness of the multi-dimensional measure of effectiveness that we have described and, second, the association of different organizational characteristics with each of these dimensions of effectiveness.

All ten hospitals had similar basic structures. In each a board of trustees was ostensibly the policy-making group, but it depended for execution of its directives on an administrator and a chief of the medical staff. These centers of power varied in their influence on hospital affairs from one hospital to another. They also varied in the degree of integration among themselves. The administrator was responsible for day-to-day operations of the hospital; he had several department heads to assist him. They included the directors of nursing, maintenance, dietary services, housekeeping, and so on. The largest staff was in the nursing department, which was responsible for around-the-clock care of patients. There were three shifts, composed of registered and practical nurses, aides, and orderlies. Each shift had a supervisor who reported to the director of nursing and supervised the work of the floor supervisors. Sections of each floor were devoted to different medical services, and team nursing was the prevalent approach in each. Only one hospital had resident physicians. All other affiliated physicians were in private practice and used the hospital facilities for their patients.

To obtain their samples of respondents, Georgopoulos and Mann stratified the hospital populations by occupational categories and selected samples within each. The sampling ratios varied from one category to another, depending upon size. All respondents completed a questionnaire administered in group sessions. In addition, the administrator, members of the board of trustees, and the chief of the medical staff were interviewed. The responses to each question were weighted by these sampling ratios to yield weighted mean-score responses

[5] For a detailed description of these hospitals and the research methods used in their study, see Georgopoulos and Mann, *op. cit.*, pp. 32-197.

[6] P. E. Mott, "Sources of Adaptation and Flexibility in Large Organizations" (Doctoral diss., The University of Michigan, 1960).

for each hospital. The hospital mean scores were ranked and rank-order correlations with selected questionnaire items were carried out.

The next opportunity for research occurred at NASA. This project was designed to test methods for effective transfer of information from social scientists to managers and was one of an extensive series of studies conducted by the Center for the Utilization of Scientific Knowledge at the University of Michigan. The author was the project director for the NASA studies and was therefore able to construct an instrument designed to test the hypotheses developed during and after the hospital study. The design called for six months of exploratory interviewing in the Office of Administration followed by mass administration of a questionnaire designed to measure the prevalence and severity of the problems discovered during the initial interviews. A long instrument was designed (see Appendix C); it included the effectiveness measures and the items that we wished to correlate with them. These data and other materials were used in training sessions with the division directors and many branch chiefs. One and a half years later a second questionnaire was administered (NASA-2) to determine whether or not certain organizational changes had taken place since the first questionnaire had been administered. Once again the effectiveness measures and other items that we wished to correlate with them were included in the questionnaire.

The Office of Administration was located at NASA headquarters in Washington, D.C. It had two basic functions: to provide certain services for headquarters and to develop various policies and procedures for administrative units in the field centers. To fulfill the first of these functions there were divisions for security, personnel, contracts, administrative services, and budgeting. Most of the remaining units were devoted to the second function. For example, there was a division responsible for developing uniform security standards for operational security units at the field centers. Similar divisions existed for financial management, management-information systems, personnel and transportation. Two units—Audit and Inspections—had NASA-wide operational responsibilities to monitor all of the centers to see that they conformed to the law, administrative orders and procedures, and so on. Although there was some interdependence among these divisions, most of their work was with outside units. Unfortunately we were prevented by contractual agreement from going outside the office to measure division effectiveness as perceived by clients.

The top managers of the next agency studied (which we shall call Alpha Agency) were promised anonymity in exchange for permission to collect and use the data from their organization, a small Federal agency with a relatively high grade structure. (Grade structure is the system by which higher grades or G.S. levels are assigned people who perform more difficult or responsible tasks. The higher the level, the higher the salary. The highest G.S. levels are managerial positions.) Despite the difference in overall grade levels, the predominant skills and objectives in this agency were in many ways similar to those in our NASA setting. There were divisions of personnel and administrative services. The professional skills of most of the people in the other units were similar to those at NASA: accounting, auditing, budgeting, and developing management-information systems. Once again we were not permitted to obtain assessments of Alpha Agency units from outside clients.

Our opportunity to obtain data from the U.S. State Department came when the Center for the Utilization of Scientific Knowledge was asked to evaluate a project that had been conducted in the administrative office (O Group) of that department. The administrative office encompassed a broader spectrum of activities than did the NASA equivalent, including some administrative guidance of certain overseas operations. We were asked by the study director whether or not we wished to include any items in the questionnaires. We submitted our effectiveness items. Unfortunately only a few of them were actually included, and the final instrument was extremely short. The questionnaires were administered en masse to all personnel within the divisions, but because of the limitations just mentioned the data are of limited usefulness to us.

Our final government research site was the Financial Management Office of the Department of Health, Education and Welfare. This office was responsible for the performance of many accounting and financial services. It contained five divisions responsible for accounting procedures, centralized payroll and travel disbursements, development of financial-management systems, and management of a data-processing center. The proportion of professionals in this organization was much lower than in the others studied because so much of the work was highly structured, as in routine payroll and voucher processing.

Data from this site were obtained by the usual methods: mass administration of questionnaires composed of closed-end items. The response rate was only 70 percent, and these data will therefore be used sparingly and cautiously. As most of the items included in the instrument involved supervisory behavior and unit effectiveness, they will be discussed almost exclusively in Chapter 7.

Identical instruments were not used at all these settings. In each we tested some new hypotheses that previous efforts had suggested. Only the effectiveness items and a few key independent variables were included throughout.

Our final research setting was a state mental hospital in Pennsylvania (Byberry). It had a reputation for the worst form of custodial care and in fact had been the subject of an article in a national magazine. The hospital was apparently hopelessly entangled in state red tape and political patronage. Patients slept in the halls in order to keep warm; requisitions to purchase sweaters, eyeglasses, and the like often did not receive approval from the state for several months. At that time (1966) there were 5500 patients, 2100 employees, and only 50 psychiatrists (including residents).

In 1966 a new administrator was appointed by Governor Raymond Shafer. His plan called for changing the role of the hospital drastically by introducing reliance on community health centers. Under this plan many patients would be discharged and treated periodically at their community health centers. Many others—particularly the senile and the regressive schizophrenics—would be transferred to smaller, private-care units. The administrator wished to measure these changes and their effects; we were commissioned to obtain before-and-after measures of a variety of organizational characteristics. Naturally, our effectiveness items were also included.

In August 1967 a questionnaire made up of closed-end items was designed and administered to treatment personnel and key administrators in the hospital. The respondents included all administrators down to and including department heads, all physicians and registered nurses, samples of practical nurses and attendants, and a 50 percent sample of para-medical personnel (psychologist, social workers, occupational therapists, and the like). Altogether 228 usable questionnaires were returned, a 90 percent response rate.

In the fall of 1968, the second measure was taken. By that time the patient census had dropped to 3900. The number of employees had risen to 2350. Most of the new staff members were social workers whose main function was to place desig-nated patients in desirable community situations. Similar sur-vey techniques were used; 230 usable questionnaires were ob-tained, an 85 percent response rate.

Table 2-2 summarizes some of our findings on the effec-tiveness items. All the scores are in the upper halves of their scales—not an unlikely result considering that all the units stud-ied were functioning. These data reveal some patterns that war-

TABLE 2-2 Mean Scores on Effectiveness Measures

	NASA-1	ALPHA AGENCY	STATE DEPARTMENT	H.E.W.	BYBERRY
Productivity index	3.69	4.00	4.09	3.47	3.86
Quantity	3.80	4.30	4.20	3.63	3.15
Quality	3.95	4.17	4.38	3.38	3.92
Efficiency	3.31	3.52	3.70	3.41	3.50
Adaptability index	3.55	3.82	*	3.67	3.74
Anticipating problems	3.33	3.37	†	3.36	3.59
Keeping up to date	3.40	3.67	†	3.45	3.60
Promptness of adjustment	3.73	4.01	4.10	4.08	3.50
Prevalence of adjustment	3.80	4.09	†	3.72	4.07
Flexibility	3.99	4.09	†	4.14	4.04
Overall effectiveness index	3.76	3.84	(3.96)§	3.66	3.82

* No index was constructed.

† This item was not included in this study.

§ No effectiveness index was constructed. The mean score shown is for a single summary item: "Overall how would you rate your division or program on effective-ness? How well does it do at fulfilling its mission or achieving its goals?"

rant discussion. The respondents at Alpha Agency, NASA, H.E.W., and Byberry believed that they were relatively most ef-fective in adjusting their routines to cope with emergencies. As-sessments of productivity and adaptability followed in that order. H.E.W. departed from the overall pattern in that evalu-ations of productivity were the lowest of those for the three effec-tiveness measures. This variation may have resulted from the newness of a payroll system that had been installed there. All these data reflect one fundamental characteristic of these and other government organizations familiar to us: They are production organizations, whether production is defined in the routine sense or as the pell-mell kind of activity required in emergencies. Routine production in government involves a vast array of activities, ranging from delivering mail and processing grant or job applications to auditing contractors and investigating alleged violations of the law. The structures of most Federal agencies reflect the classic scientific-administration model of organization, with its emphasis on detailed procedures to govern the flow of work. Millions of dollars have been spent to design procedures for typing, filing, and routing, which are thus fundamentally similar in all government offices. Clearly, considerable thought and effort have been devoted to achieving acceptable production levels and techniques.

But political considerations supersede those of production at all times, and government agencies are geared to deliver whatever is necessary to facilitate the political objectives of the President, his political executives, the Congress, and powerful private citizens. They are flexible. If the Soviet Union has forged ahead in space technology, a new agency with double-time marching orders is created. If the President makes a speech suggesting that he wishes to clean up urban slums, then a program to achieve this objective must be mounted rapidly. Flexibility is also necessary because politically sensitive issues or issues that might be embarrassing to the agency itself must be handled rapidly before they are discovered by reporters, the Government Accounting Office, or any of a number of other groups. Highly selective responsiveness to letters of inquiry from congressmen, requests from agency administrators, and speeches by the President is the most impressive characteristic of Federal agencies. Usually such requests are politically or administratively important, but sometimes they are not; nevertheless the agencies usually respond.

So common and accepted are such demands for flexibility that unreasonable pressure to perform is not related to the overall effectiveness of the divisions studied here ($r = -.08$ in NASA-1, $-.12$ in NASA-2, and $-.04$ in Alpha Agency). This finding is quite different from that of Georgopoulos and Mann, who showed that, the higher were the perceived amounts of unreasonable pressure, the lower was the quality of patient care.[7] Much apparently depends upon the person's expectations and the types of cognitive adjustment that he makes. As one NASA professional put it, "Sure, we get lots of unreasonable pressure, but it is *positive* unreasonable pressure."

This penchant for flexibility explains why the respondents in all agencies uniformly rated the efficiency of their units relatively low. Efficiency simply did not have the priority that prompt completion had. In one sense the processes of government are ever new. New programs are initiated, and old ones sometimes fade; new political executives shift previous priorities. In order for administrations to reap the political rewards of these new efforts, agencies must move rapidly first and efficiently second.

There are other reasons for the relatively low appraisal of efficiency; all but one of them are idiosyncratic. The one exception is demands by Congress and the executives for accountability. Present-day government employees wear hair shirts woven during the civil-service reform movement that began in the late 1800s. To ensure honesty and a certain amount of rationality in performance, detailed procedural rules were adopted for government employees. These rules have undoubtedly increased accountability and honesty, but they have also slowed the work process. To maintain high production standards in the face of current demands requires larger staffs than would otherwise be necessary.

Perhaps the reasons that the divisions studied scored relatively low on the adaptability index, particularly on certain parts of it, are now clearer. These divisions did poorly in the more symbolic aspects of adaptation—anticipating problems and keeping abreast of new techniques and tools—and better in such behavioral aspects as prompt and prevalent adjustment to changes in routines. The latter performance reflects their customary compliance with the demands of management, the former their role in the system. Departments and agencies are designed as productive organizations. The political figures in the White House and Congress usually consider the anticipation of major problems and the creation of new solutions to such problems their own responsibility. They thus customarily surround themselves with creative people

[7] Georgopoulos and Mann, *op. cit.*, p. 398.

whose ideas they can translate into action and, not coincidentally, into political advantage. To some extent those who head Federal agencies and departments share in this creative process but to a far lesser degree than is generally recognized. They soon find themselves responding to one pressure after another. They also find that they cannot surround themselves with adequate numbers of "idea men" because Congress, fearing the potential power of the agencies, has sharply limited the staffs of most department and agency heads. One agency head said in ill-disguised exasperation, "If you can find a way for me to hide a planning staff from Congress, let me know." It is remarkable that some agency heads accomplish as much as they do.

Only four of our effectiveness items were included in the study of the ten hospitals: quality of production, promptness and prevalence of adjustment to change, and flexibility. The pattern of responses to these items was different from that in the government agencies. The highest self-appraisals by professional and administrative members of the hospital staff were on the two measures of behavioral adaptation. On the index of prevalence of adaptation the hospital mean scores for the ten hospitals were almost identical with those for promptness of adaptation, ranging from 4.39 to 4.08—well above the self-appraisals obtained in government agencies. This finding probably reflects two facts about hospitals: First, they are centers for the diffusion of new knowledge about medical and nursing techniques, drugs, and instruments and, second, their staffs feel a strong need to adapt new techniques when there is the slightest possibility that they will save the lives of patients. The second highest level of performance was on the quality of patient care, the hospital means ranged from 4.01 to 3.06.[8] The lowest mean scores were on flexibility, but they were only slightly lower than those for quality of patient care. Nevertheless, they were considerably lower than were the corresponding scores for the government agencies in this study.

SUMMARY

Organizational effectiveness has been defined as the ability of an organization to mobilize its centers of power to produce, adapt to change, and cope with emergencies. The first two of these activities have been divided to permit refined measurement by means of questionnaire items administered at all our research sites. Validity studies (see Appendix A) of the effectiveness measures were encouraging enough to warrant continued use, though some limitations were discovered. If for any reason the respondents were using other than modern professional criteria for evaluating the performances of their work groups, the results of their evaluations would not be valid. Some protection against this possibility could be ensured by comparing the evaluations of people within the target group with similar evaluations by outsiders whose work brings them in contact with the target group.

We are aware that more validity studies should be conducted, but we do think that subjective assessments are promising even now. Our studies suggest one modification in the method of measuring effectiveness: The item measuring the extent to which members keep abreast of new tools and methods of work should be dropped from the adaptability measure. Two questions designed to obtain more detailed assessments of the symbolic adaptability of an organization—that is, the adequacy of its problem-solving processes—should be substituted. Specifically, we need measures of the range of solutions available to solve problems and of the efficiency with which a solution is selected from those offered. These changes have been made in a current study of the Social and Rehabilitation Service of H.E.W. Although such changes are theoretically important, our preliminary analyses of the S.R.S. data suggest that they have little, if any, effect on how the index of adaptability is related to key independent variables. This follow-up study will appear in a later report.

3
Relating Characteristics
of Organizations
to Their Effectiveness

In this chapter some of the more pervasive organizational properties—coordination, communication, levels of staff skills,
integration, and so on—will be examined in relation to organizational effectiveness. The most notable exceptions are
power, authority, and decision-making structures, which will
be discussed in Chapter 4. Furthermore, certain cultural and
social-psychological ·characteristics that occur throughout
organizations—for example, identification with goals and extent
to which expectations are shared—are also examined here.

There is a considerable literature on the correlates of
productivity, adaptability, and flexibility, but as in so many
other areas of sociology, it is crammed with contradictory
findings. A classic example is the many attempts to relate productivity and job satisfaction. Some early findings showed
the two to be related, and on this foundation certain industrial
social scientists have constructed whole programs for the management of men. Ensuing studies produced contradictions,
however. Productivity was found to be negatively related
or sometimes simply unrelated to job satisfaction. One of the
most persistent investigators of this problem finally concluded,
"I would like to begin by asserting, without qualification, that
productivity and job satisfaction do not necessarily go together."[1] Similar conclusions can be reached for other variables
in relation to productivity, adaptability, and flexibility.

We have reviewed all the studies that we could find in
which attempts were made to relate aspects of organizational
effectiveness to other organizational characteristics. No pattern

[1]Robert L. Kahn, "Productivity and Job Satisfaction," *Personnel Psychology* 13 (1960): 275.

other than contradiction emerged. One study might show a positive relationship between two variables, another no relationship, and a third a negative one. But we are also struck by the dissimilarities among the settings in which these earlier studies were conducted, for they varied greatly in degree of closure. Some involved teams of scientists or executives, whereas others involved railroad or assembly-line workers. The amounts of adaptation and improvisation required of people in these different settings varied greatly, as did the interfaces between roles and groups. Suppose that measures of these organizational properties had been included in earlier studies? Would the contradiction in findings have been avoided? Although such questions cannot be answered, the hypotheses of some of these studies were tested in some of the research settings included in our study.

HYPOTHESES ABOUT PRODUCTIVE ORGANIZATIONS
Our reasoning led to the following hypotheses:

A. When task structuring is high, productivity is positively related to
   1. Formal coordination
   2. Levels of workers' skills
   3. Conditions for achieving negotiated orders
   4. Clarity of and adherence to rules governing work

B. When task structuring is high, productivity is not necessarily related to
   1. Managerial awareness of problems
   2. Managerial success at solving problems
   3. Perceptions about the reasonableness and empathy of top management (rational-trust)
   4. Clarity of objectives

C. When task structuring is high, productivity is negatively related to
   1. Interunit conflict
   2. Conflicting priorities

D. When task structuring is low, productivity is related to
   1. Formal coordination
   2. Conditions for achieving negotiated orders
      a. coordination by avoidance

      b. problem solving at lower echelons

      c. ease in exchanging ideas and information

    3. Levels of workers' skills

    4. Clarity of objectives

E. When task structuring is low, productivity is not necessarily related to

    1. Managerial awareness of problems

    2. Managerial success at solving problems

F. When task structuring is low, productivity is negatively related to

    1. Interunit conflict

    2. Conflicting priorities

It is assumed that intertask structuring or formal and informal coordination, as well as levels of skills, are the major predictors of effective production, which is usually a closed-system activity. Coordination involves articulation of the parts according to some organizing principle. Without it the rhythms of activities in the various centers of power would not be meshed; with it the activities of the parts are linked together in a meaningful whole.[2] The interfaces among selected centers of power, which are basically influence relationships, become organized: stable, consistent, and often ordered in a hierarchy. Coordination as an activity involves the creation of rules specifying who will do what, when, and at what level of performance: creation or modification of formal influence structures.

Production requires that people or things undergo a series of experiences that modify them in some desired way. This series of experiences has an inherent logic (though there is often more than one acceptable way to produce something), which varies in definiteness, predictability, and degree of integration. If the sequence is definite, predictable, and highly integrated formal coordination will suffice. Such coordination involves a comprehensive plan for articulating the parts of the organization and detailed specification of routines (programs) for each part and for each role in that part. It thus involves the closed-system, structuring approach discussed in Chapter 1. We have argued, however, that the characteristics of some tasks do not lend themselves to complete structuring. In such instances there

---

[2]Basil S. Georgopoulos and Floyd C. Mann, *The Community General Hospital* (New York: Macmillan, 1962).

is greater need for decentralization and improvisation during the production process, for informal coordination through negotiated orders. The ratio of formally specified to informally negotiated acts of coordination decreases. The negotiated order manifests itself when members avoid creating problems for one another, develop necessary channels of communication to exchange ideas and information, and solve the adaptive problems inherent in productive activity.

Repeated managerial involvement in the solution of production problems is symptomatic of ineffective production. Except for major problems that require changes in basic policies or the use of resources that only top management has the authority to allocate, all others should be solved at the lowest possible levels, where rapid decisions can be made by people who are intimately familiar with the circumstances. When such problems are referred to higher levels of management, delays are inevitable. When task structuring is appropriately high there is almost no need for managerial problem solving because the system is closed, and by definition very little adaptation is required. Therefore we expect to find no relationship whatever between managerial problem solving and productivity.

The value of clear objectives at the unstructured end of the continuum has already been discussed. They provide direction in the negotiation of order. When tasks are highly structured clear objectives serve no useful function other than helping to rationalize the environment for workers. On the other hand, clear rules and guidelines are essential in highly structured situations because they are key means of structuring tasks. In less structured situations they help to integrate the parts of the organization that must work together.

The major symptom of failure in formal coordination or in negotiating orders is conflict at the interface. Such conflict less often takes the form of anger, resentment, or related affective states than it appears as disagreement about how to structure interface relations. Problems between different units can lead to this type of conflict unless they are solved promptly and satisfactorily. Problems that recur cause frustration and a tendency to blame the people in the other unit. When frustration at the interface builds up to hostility, which replaces emphasis on problem solving, members of the involved units will go out of their way to create problems for each other, rather than avoiding them. The climate for negotiating orders is destroyed, hostility escalates, and productive goals are no longer served.

Basil S. Georgopoulos and Floyd C. Mann found significant negative relationships between interdepartmental tension and quality of patient care.[3] We expect that it similarly affects the quantity and efficiency of production. Efficiency is most sensitive to failures in coordination because the amounts of resources used may be increased. Both quantity and quality of production can be maintained despite failures in coordination by allocating additional resources: overtime, additional personnel, and so on. Such correctives add to the input and reduce the efficiency of production. Quality is the next most likely aspect of production to be affected by coordination problems. The requirements for quality are generally *additional* to those for quantity. More things must be done to the product, and therefore greater demands are placed on the coordinating system—provided that the product requires the inputs of more than one subgroup.

Productivity, as we noted earlier, is a function of coordination and levels of skills. These variables are not independent of each other or, as indicated, of the degree of task structuring in the production process. Inherent in every plan for coordination is a unique requirement for skill levels. For example, the single-wing formation in football requires higher levels of skills than does the T formation. In the former one player must excel at running, passing, and kicking, whereas in the T formation these activities are divided among all the members of the backfield. In hospitals that sort patients into different units according to the amount of care they need (intensive care to self-care units), a smaller proportion of skilled nurses are required than in hospitals with mixed care units because they permit concentration of the most skilled nurses in the intensive care units. To exceed the levels of skills adds little to productivity and can reduce morale if people are continuously performing below their levels of competence. A surplus of talent is useful, however, for the identification and development of potential supervisory and managerial personnel.

Finally, we have proposed a relationship between the

[3] *Ibid.*, p. 398.

rational-trust characteristics of leaders and productivity, and that concept must now be explained. We type leaders according to their positions relative to any given individual in the organization: near, intermediate, and remote. Leaders who were near could have considerable control over their subordinates, but their very proximity permitted subordinates to test hypotheses about them. Remote leaders seldom had as much control of, or direct impact on, a person's work, and consequently employees were less motivated to know what they were like. The intermediate leader, who was usually only two or three steps up the hierarchy, presented a special problem. He was far enough removed to be seldom, if ever, visible, yet he was sufficiently close so that the worker sensed his significant influence over his own work. The worker wanted to know what he was like, and in the absence of genuine data he generated them himself and operated as if they were true. The leader might be perceived as trustworthy, just, and rational; as capricious, malevolent, cold, and conspiratorial; or as any of hundreds of other combinations. We shall label a person with the first complex of traits a "rational-trust leader."[4] The rational-trust leader is believed, first, to be aware of the points of view, needs, and problems of those who work for him and to take them into account (not necessarily to agree with them) when he makes decisions; second, to make fair, rational decisions, usually based on established and known criteria; and, third, to conform in his behavior to known standards.

We expect individuals to be most comfortable and loyal in this rational atmosphere of trust, which promotes morale and cohesiveness. It has already been suggested that certain types of managerial behaviors like problem solving have little or no relation to productivity. Management is essentially an adaptive activity. In fact, we anticipate that much of what management does, by its very nature, interferes with production. But the rational-trust atmosphere may slightly assist productivity, for workers in such an atmosphere may more readily accept production objectives set by remote leaders. Without this atmosphere there is no reason to assume that workers with high morale and team spirit will translate it into productive behavior.

[4] This basic idea comes from Guy E. Swanson, Professor of Sociology, University of California, Berkeley; we have changed the label and modified the content somewhat.

FINDINGS ON PRODUCTIVITY

At the National Aeronautics and Space Administration a panel of five judges who were particularly well acquainted with the twelve divisions included in our study were asked to assess the average degree of task structuring in each of forty branches within these divisions.[5] Ordinarily each large division was divided into four branches. The technique used was F. Fiedler's modification of M. E. Shaw's approach,[6] which involved ranking each branch on four dimensions of structure: clarity of goals, multiplicity of paths to goals, verifiability of decisions, and specificity of solutions. Altogether thirty-four branches were rated (the panel was not sufficiently familiar with six of the branches to rate them). The average rank-order correlation among the five raters was .60 ($n = 34$, $p < .01$). The task score assigned to each branch was the average of its scores by the five raters.

To test the effects of structure each respondent in the thirty-four branches was assigned the average task score of his branch. The resulting distribution of scores was divided into three categories (see Chapter 7, note 10), high, medium, and low. Correlations between productivity and the independent variables were carried out within each of these three categories. The results are shown in Table 3-1.

The branches of NASA that had the most highly structured tasks were the motor pool, the mail room, the accounting data processors, and the personnel action processors, but none of these branches came anywhere near the theoretical extreme of structuring. Some branches did come quite near the other extreme, however; they included groups and individuals whose work could be performed in many different ways, involving frequent and long phases of improvisation (investigations, audits, and creation of management-information and financial-management systems).

The data generally supported our hypotheses. When task structuring was low most measures of organizational and normative integration were highly and significantly correlated

---

[5] For details of the procedure, see D. Anthony Butterfield, "An Integrative Approach to the Study of Leadership Effectiveness in Organizations" (Doctoral diss., The University of Michigan, 1968) p. 59.

[6] See F. Fiedler, *A Theory of Leadership Effectiveness* (New York: McGraw-Hill, 1967), pp. 25-28; and M. E. Shaw, "Scaling Group Tasks: A Method for Dimensional Analysis," mimeographed (Gainesville: University of Florida, 1963).

TABLE 3-1 *Relationships Between Productivity and Other Organizational Characteristics for Different Degrees of Task Structure*

MEASURES OF ORGANIZATIONAL CHARACTERISTICS	TASK STRUCTURE		
	HIGH	MEDIUM	LOW
Clarity of normative environment			
Clarity of objectives toward which to work	.01	.45	.47
Clarity of rules, policies, and guidelines	.29	.29	.29
Intertask structure (coordination)			
How well related jobs are meshed to achieve objectives	.25	.44	.49
Extent to which independent assignments are well planned	.31	.33	.54
Conditions for negotiating orders			
Ease of exchanging ideas and information with others doing related work	.18	.31	.53
Extent to which people doing related work avoid creating problems for one another	.34	.28	.43
How well coordination problems with others doing related work are handled	.40	.42	.58
Levels of skills			
Proportion of personnel competent to do the division's work	.31	.29	.49
Rational-trust relationship			
Index of rational-trust items	.16	.18	.16
N	50	97	107
Product-moment correlations			
r significant at .05 level	.28	.20	.19
r significant at .01 level	.37	.26	.25

with productivity. The exception was the rational-trust index, which was unrelated to productivity. We had not expected a very high correlation because rational-trust leadership had its primary impact on certain intervening variables like team spirit, identification with NASA, and morale, but we did expect a greater effect than we obtained.

Where tasks were highly structured the relationships were also about as expected. The correlations were relatively low. Clarity of objectives was not related to the index of productivity and clarity of rules, policies, and guidelines was barely related to it. Similarly, measures of coordination and of conditions for negotiating orders were only very modestly related to productivity. Even the measure of levels of skills of personnel was only modestly related to effective productivity. Obviously, if tasks are highly structured, these organizational characteristics contribute very little to achieving high productivity.

We turn now to examination of the data from settings where measures of task structure were not obtained.

Ten Hospitals

It is our impression that the routine care of patients at most of the ten hospitals in this study was about in the lower middle of the continuum of task structuring. The work of key administrative personnel and physicians was less structured. In their analyses of these hospitals Georgopoulos and Mann found that the quality of patient care was related positively to levels of skills, specifically to the relative proportions of registered and practical nurses on the nursing staff; positively to formal coordination; negatively to interdepartmental tension and conflict; and positively to the degree that expectations were shared by physicians and nurses.[7] Three further points emerged from reanalysis of the data. First, most elements of the negotiated orders were not related to the quality of overall care, but most were positively related to the quality of nursing care. Second, the degree to which the hospital administrators and directors of nursing were aware of problems and skilled in solving them was not related to the quality of overall care given. Third, clarity of rules was not related to the quality of overall care, but the extent to which people adhered to these rules was positively related.

These findings support our hypotheses. The negotiated order was not as important in quality of production in semistructured situations as it might have been in less structured ones. Formal coordination and skill levels were the most powerful predictors of effectiveness in patient care. In fact, a first-order correlation relating these two dimensions to quality of care was highly significant ($r_s = .87$, $p < .01$). It appears that the most effective hospitals were those that had achieved the greatest task and intertask structuring in the activities of nurses, aides, and orderlies. There was then little need for managerial involvement in the production process, as reflected in the lack of correlation between managerial problem-solving abilities and quality of care.

Federal Agency Data

Very few of the Federal employees who participated in our studies did work that was even fairly structured. The exceptions were the administrative services personnel in NASA and Alpha Agency, the keypunch operators in one branch of NASA,

[7] Georgopoulos and Mann, *op. cit.*, pp. 365-421.

and a few other semiskilled personnel. When we use G.S. level as a criterion of structure, we find that at most twenty-five of the NASA respondents and eleven from Alpha Agency (6 and 3 percent respectively) had very highly structured jobs. In addition some clerks and lower-level typists did fairly structured work. Although we do not have the same detailed familiarity with the work of our respondents in the State Department, the units in which they worked were functionally similar to those in NASA that were included in this study. We therefore, expected that the proportion of State Department respondents doing highly structured work would be similar to that in NASA; the operative hypotheses would then have been those for less structured work situations. Table 3-2 shows the relationships among the measures designed to test many of these hypotheses.

The measures of formal coordination were highly related to those of production as were the measures of levels of skills and conditions for negotiating order. The State Department data supported these findings: Quantity, quality, and efficiency of production were correlated (r = .43, .42, and .49 respectively)[8] with the meshing of related jobs to achieve organizational objectives. The correlation between efficiency and coordination was higher in all the government studies than were those between the other two productivity measures and coordination. The average correlations with coordination for all four sites were r = .39, .43, and .51 for quantity, quality, and efficiency respectively, thus providing some confirmation for the hypothesis that higher levels of coordination are required to achieve efficient functioning than are required to achieve quantity production. The individual items on the rational-trust index were more highly related to productivity in NASA than was the index itself (r = .10). The top-management group that respondents were asked to describe constituted the level immediately above the division directors. When these items were combined in a single index and correlated with job satisfaction and team spirit, significant results (r = .30 in both instances, significant beyond the .01 level) were obtained. Undoubtedly many people ascribed these characteristics to top management because they were satisfied with their jobs and because they had esprit de corps, but the opposite explanation deserves more attention than it has received in

---

[8] These correlations are all significant beyond the .01 level.

TABLE 3-2 Organizational Characteristics and Productivity

MEASURES OF ORGANIZATIONAL CHARACTERISTICS	INDEX OF PRODUCTIVITY		
	NASA-1	NASA-2	ALPHA AGENCY
Clarity of normative environment			
Clarity of objectives toward which to work	.29*	.42	.36
Clarity of rules, policies, and guidelines	.21	†	.27
Extent to which workers are given conflicting priorities		−.05	.00
Extent to which front office changes policies without advance notice	−.26		
Intertask structure (coordination)			
How well related jobs are meshed to achieve objectives	.48	.59	.51
Extent to which independent assignments are well planned	.40		
Conditions for negotiating orders			
Ease of exchanging ideas and information with others doing related work	.38	.39	.31
Extent to which people doing related work avoid creating problems for one another	.38	.39	.33
How well coordination problems with others doing related work are handled	.49	.51	.45
Levels of skills			
Proportion of personnel competent to do the division's work	.42		.43
Rational-trust relationship			
Extent to which front office is perceived as following its own rules	.21		
Extent to which front office is perceived as understanding workers' needs, problems, and points of view	.30		
Extent to which top management is perceived as fair and reasonable	.21		.16

* Pearson product-moment correlations were used. $N > 375$ in all cases; $r = .10$, $p < .05$; $r = .13$, $p < .01$.

† When no correlation coefficient appears, the variable was not included in that particular study.

the literature. When managers are perceived as rational and trustworthy, employees are more likely to develop a sense of identification and esprit with their work groups. Or when managers are perceived as malevolent, capricious, and insensitive, every order is viewed with suspicion, and few people enjoy working for them.

There was a smaller correlation between the single rational-trust item [9] included in the study of Alpha Agency and pro-

[9] To what extent are the people in the Director's Office fair and reasonable in their decisions that affect your work, regardless of whether those decisions are favorable to you or not?

ductivity. But this correlation was undoubtedly lower because of the lack of variability in the rational-trust item; very few people selected the least favorable options (the mean score was 4.22 on a 5-point scale). The director and the deputy director were almost universally considered fair and reasonable in their decisions. Controlling for G.S. level did not change the picture; the same distribution of responses was obtained at every G.S. level. In NASA the attribution of rational-trust characteristics was also uniform by level, with the exception of G.S. levels 11-13, at which evaluations were somewhat less positive.

When rational trust existed in NASA, employees were also very likely to report easy communication with people in the front office (r = .42, p < .01) and satisfaction with the amounts of information received from that office (r = .36, p < .01). Again these relationships are likely to have worked in two ways: Rational trust reduced the barriers to communication and enabled individuals to test their perceptions.

Our measures of the clarity of objectives and norms generally supported our hypotheses. Clarity of objectives was related to productivity at both Alpha Agency and NASA. In unstructured work situations clear objectives helped individuals to make decisions about directions in which to work. Clear rules also enabled workers to proceed with minimum false starts. Surprisingly, however, conflicting priorities showed no relation to productivity, though we had expected a very high negative correlation. It may be that when professionals in these organizations were confronted with conflicting priorities they simply tried to meet them all. We have some impression that this explanation is correct at least for the occasions when a crash-program aura pervaded even the administrative sections of the organization.

As clear objectives and policies augment productivity, unexpected changes in them are detrimental to it. Such changes were a frequent complaint at NASA, where respondents reported that they usually learned of policy changes only after their work had progressed so far that it had to be altered when it came to the attention of people who already knew about the change. Time was thus lost on false starts.

Our measures of interdivisional tension in NASA-1 were rewarding from one point of view and dissatisfying from another. They were rewarding in that they revealed almost no tension, conflict, or friction among the divisions. No division received a mean tension score as high as 2.00 ("little tension"), a result primarily of the low interdependence among the divisions and of fairly steady efforts at cooperation. As there was little variation in this measure, however, it could not be related as expected to the measure of productivity ($r = -.12$). It was related in the predicted direction to the measure of overall effectiveness ($r = -.21$, $p < .01$) and was highly related to the measure of outside evaluations of effectiveness ($r = .43$, $p < .01$). As division productivity was so little a function of cooperation with other divisions, this result is not surprising.

Byberry-1

The productivity items were included in the Byberry-1 study, which permitted construction of our productivity index. This index was correlated ($r = .47$, $p < .01$) with an item on the extent to which the staff was successful at making patients comfortable.

Only a few of the independent variables already discussed were included in the Byberry-1 study, but four items designed to measure the clarity of the normative environment and its relationship with productivity were included: clarity of the objectives toward which to work ($r = .33$), clarity of hospital policies and guidelines ($r = .13$), how well duties and responsibilities were defined ($r = .31$), and frequency with which different priorities for work were assigned ($r = -.30$). Most of these items were related as expected to productivity; the exception was that on clarity of hospital policies and guidelines. This study was the first in which this item had not shared a significant amount of variance. Also for the first time there was no strong correlation between the timing of activities in everyday routine ($r = .21$).

Perhaps these findings can be explained in the light of work processes in a hospital devoted to custodial care of long-term patients. In such settings there are activities that must be coordinated. Patients must receive drugs, bathing and eating schedules must be maintained, and so forth. But the number and frequency of such activities are considerably less than in hospitals devoted to medical care of short-term patients. At Byberry the nursing supervisor for each building spent most of her time in her office, and the attendants worked with the patients, whose own responsibilities were really minimal. In fact, it appeared that the patients spent much of their time simply sitting in common rooms. So great was their sensory deprivation that the arrival of the barber was an exciting event. It is possible, therefore, that measures of formal coordination were not related to productivity because there was little need for formal coordination. In this custodial institution most activities, particularly among attendants, were initiated in response to patient's needs, rather than by the hospital staffs. Attendants received rather simple training; their roles involved a few formally specified activities and were highly routine. In the Byberry-2 study we asked to what extent the respondents' jobs were routine; 72 percent of the attendants and 42 percent of the nurses replied that "Almost all of their work is routine" or that "It is more routine than not." When there are ample opportunities to make ad hoc arrangements (to negotiate orders) the standards of custodial care can be met.

One measure of conditions for negotiating orders—ease of exchanging ideas and information with others doing related work—was included in this study. It was correlated ($r = .47$, $p < .01$) with measures of productivity. Our explanation is mainly speculative, but it does suggest an interesting hypothesis: When task structuring is high, need for interdependence is slight, and level of technology is low, productivity may be a function of role training, role clarity, and the ability to negotiate orders when they are needed. It also seems that the supervisor's role should be especially crucial in the achievement of unified direction when horizontal interdependence is so low. The data supported this expectation. The supervisor's ability to solve problems as perceived by his subordinates was correlated ($r = .46$) with productivity. In fact, almost all the supervisory items were similarly correlated with productivity. As we shall show in Chapter 7, this pattern of high relationships between productivity and supervisory behavior was unusual at our research sites.

A similar pattern (except that task structuring was low) occurred in one division of NASA, no relationship between horizontal coordination (or communication) and productivity was found. The division comprised a number of specialists working independently on the design of management-information systems. There, too, the supervisor's activities were essential to the achievement of high productivity. Items measuring his availability to subordinates, his willingness to give advice and solve problems, and his performance of administrative functions were highly correlated with productivity in the division.

Summary of Findings on Productivity

The data on productivity generally supported our hypotheses. In the more structured atmosphere of the hospital for short-term patients productivity was mainly a function of formal coordination and level skills. For the less structured tasks of the government divisions studied the existence of a climate conducive to negotiating orders rivaled levels of skills and formal coordination in importance for productivity. In the same setting the presence of an aura of rational trust around managers a few steps removed in the hierarchy seemed only modestly related to productivity, but managerial intervention in the productive process and failure to communicate policy changes in advance did not facilitate routine production. The managerial behavior that was related to productivity and to effectiveness in general will be discussed in Chapters 6 and 7.

HYPOTHESES ABOUT ADAPTIVE ORGANIZATIONS

As with production, it is useful to distinguish among styles of adaptation by the degree of task structure involved. The adaptive process can be highly structured, as in programmed innovations in some major chemical companies and automobile design and engineering years before actual marketing of the products. This form of adaptation resembles production because it is produced by linking in a logical series of preconceived and highly structured processes. At the other end of the continuum adaptation involves considerable improvisation. Examples from our research settings are abundant, for many of the professionals in these agencies were involved in project work; that is, they were given complex problems to solve and were expected to develop and recommend solutions. Typical problems were how to transport booster rockets to Cape Kennedy, what accounting procedures should be used to record medical expenditures, how to reduce the personnel turnover rate at a certain center. When there were few precedents for these problems, solutions were developed through processes involving phases of symbolic adaptation meshed with phases of production. In social-science research, for instance, problem-solving involves linking phases of symbolic adaptation with such productive activities as sampling, coding, and keypunching. The adaptive task is less structured when it involves fewer, shorter, and more innovative productive phases. Unfortunately, at none of the sites that we studied was a more structured form of adaptability prevalent.

Our general hypothesis was that both symbolic and behavioral adaptability is most likely to occur in highly integrated organizations. This hypothesis was expected to apply to all adaptive tasks, regardless of their degree of structure. The factors that contribute to integration were the independent variables in our studies:

A. Horizontal integration
   1. Formal coordination
   2. Informal coordination through negotiating orders
B. Hierarchical integration
   1. Integration of leadership
   2. Managerial awareness of and ability to solve problems
   3. Rational-trust status
C. Cultural and social-psychological integration
   1. Clear objectives
   2. Clear rules that are adhered to
   3. Shared expectation systems
   4. Strong team spirit

Horizontal Integration

Much of the literature on social and organizational change can be invoked to support claims of a relationship between adaptability and integration.[10] It is clear, for example, that if behavioral adaptability is to occur people must learn what they are expected to do differently. Some communication among the parts is therefore required. John and Elaine Cumming[11] demonstrated this necessity in their study of a large mental hospital whose staff exhibited high resistance to change. Closer inspection revealed that the staff was highly

---

[10] P. E. Mott, "Sources of Adaptation and Flexibility in Large Organizations" (Doctoral diss., The University of Michigan, 1960).

[11] John Cumming and Elaine Cumming, "Social Equilibrium and Social Change in the Large Mental Hospital," in *The Patient and the Mental Hospital*, ed. M. Greenblatt, D. Levinson, and R. Williams (New York: Free Press, 1957), pp. 51-76.

segmented; departmental lines cut vertically and professional lines cut horizontally. The people in each segment guarded their boundaries zealously and communications from one segment seldom penetrated or produced the desired effects in others. And, as so often happens when such segmentation exists, interface conflict was high. Ronald Lippitt, J. Watson, and B. Westley concisely summarized the consequences: "Once they are established these barriers seem not only self-perpetuating but self-aggravating. Defensive responses, distorted perceptions, and mutual antagonisms come to characterize the relationships between the subparts."[12] Under these conditions changes affecting more than one segment were virtually impossible to implement because any change originating in one segment would not be accepted in the others. Robert S. Fox, R. Lippitt, and Richard A. Schmuck found that they could predict to which classrooms a new teaching technique would spread, depending upon whether the other classrooms were isolated from or integrated with the one in which the technique originated, adaptation thus followed clique lines.[13] Elliott Jaques called this situation "maladaptive segmentation" and claimed that it could be rectified through development of an interunit communications structure, shared expectations, and consensus on the value of a positive negotiated order.[14] The Cummings found that their first task was to establish a functioning communications network along which all subsequent messages about change could travel. No one change can produce an integrated organization, however. The Cummings, for example, found it necessary to centralize power somewhat in order to obtain compliance with their orders. Formal coordination is also important because it links roles and can minimize conflict among groups that must work together.

Problems vary in their scope and significance. Major problems requiring pervasive adjustments usually undergo high-level staff analyses in the initial phases of symbolic adapta-

[12]Ronald Lippitt, J. Watson, and B. Westley, *The Dynamics of Planned Change* (New York: Harcourt Brace Jovanovich, 1958), p. 47.

[13] Robert S. Fox, Ronald Lippitt, and Richard A. Schmuck, *Pupil-Teacher Adjustment and Mutual Adaptation in Creating Classroom Learning Environments*, (Ann Arbor: Institute for Social Research, The University of Michigan, 1964).

[14] Elliott Jaques, *The Changing Culture of a Factory* (New York; Holt, Rinehart and Winston, 1952), p. 305.

tion and later implementation programs for behavioral adaptation. But there are countless intermediate and minor problems that cannot receive this sort of attention. These problems are nevertheless important because of the sheer number of them and because of their inevitable impacts on production. Frequently it is sufficient, even necessary, to solve them informally, to negotiate informal orders. If adaptability is to be high, it is essential that organizational conditions foster negotiated orders: People should be free to improvise solutions to problems, should come together easily to exchange ideas and propose solutions, and should unilaterally avoid creating problems for one another.

Hierarchical Integration

Our evidence on productivity confirmed that management's role in productive activities was minimal except when task interdependence was low. Close supervision by managers can be dysfunctional in production. In effective organizations in which some task and intertask structuring existed management was almost exclusively involved in adaptive activities. When we review studies that have linked management behavior to organizational performance, we find that the great majority have focused on adaptive rather than productive aspects of performance, even though it was often assumed that both were being studied. Management must be involved in adaptive processes because its members are often the only ones with adequate authority and resources to make the decisions or changes required. Also, because of their positions, they often use a broader range of criteria for problem solving than do lower level personnel. Political and social factors may loom as important or more important than purely technical ones. Their positions also give them access to more alternative solutions than their subordinates.

Leaders also play a vital role in achieving and maintaining organizational cohesion. When leadership is shared but segmented, then vertical segmentation among units is likely. But an integrated elite can ensure integration of units and prompt and prevalent acceptance of change; the potential deviant has difficulty finding a segment in which his deviance will be accepted. By solving problems of coordination before they become disruptive and by maintaining the conditions for developing negotiated orders managers sustain cohesion. Finally, we expect that when intermediate leaders have high rational-trust status, organizational adaptation will be greater. When intermediate leaders are considered reasonable, fair, and willing to take the views of others into account, workers are more willing to accept the changes in routines initiated by these leaders and more likely to inform them of organizational problems.

Cultural and Social-Psychological Integration

The existence of a clear set of objectives fosters adaptation for two reasons. First, objectives can provide directions for problem solving, so that adaptation can be geared to collective purposes. Second, as we have already noted, clear, viable objectives help individuals to understand the organizations in which they work. They can interpret managerial behavior in the light of these objectives and can thus render their environments more rational and certain. They are then more likely to exhibit greater sensitivity and concern for assisting the unit to achieve its objectives. (Clear rules that are generally adhered to have a similar impact.)

Identification with collective objectives does not, however, necessarily further adaptations.[15] A person may identify with the organization and its objectives and still have reasons for resisting changes in his own routine. He may identify with objectives yet disagree with the prescribed means for achieving them. He may also identify with the organization itself, forming strong attachments to the present structure, layout, and facilities; he is then a traditionalist, rather than an innovator.

The importance of shared expectation systems in integration has already been discussed in connection with the mitigation of conflict and the development of empathy. Such systems promote integration by permitting easy exchange of ideas and information, which is essential to the adaptive process. When these positive cultural and psychological conditions exist and individuals to some extent identify with the people with whom they work, negotiated orders will function well, and resistance to change will be minimal.

[15] Herbert A. Simon, *Administrative Behavior* (New York: Macmillan, 1951), p. 206.

Levels of Skill and Experience

In addition to the various types of integration there are other organizational characteristics that affect adaptability. Formal coordination and levels of skill are as necessary for programmed adaptation as for programmed production. There is little point to exceeding the level of skills required; it is wasteful to have a chemist with a Ph.D. degree doing nothing more than dozens of titrations every day or a comparably qualified sociologist doing nothing but coding routine survey data. But, as demands for improvisation increase, the levels of skill required also increase. Therefore no necessary relationship between the proportion of professional workers in an organization and its adaptability can be expected.[16] Furthermore, professionals can create adaptation problems, for they will concur with some changes in their routines yet resist others for reasons that can be traced to their professional training. Many professionals ritualize their methods and narrow the range of problems that they consider relevant. As their techniques become outmoded and the relevance of certain problems to our dynamic society lessens, their adherence to them can reduce the adaptability of the organization. When such professionals achieve positions of leadership, they may resist the introduction of new routines in their units. We expect that the higher the proportion of professionals with long service in leadership positions, the less adaptive the organization will be.

The Permanence of Physical Structures

A building is often constructed in accordance with a comprehensive work plan. If the interior structure is inflexible, changes in this plan or in work routines are difficult. In addition, older buildings are more likely to have older staffs with longer service, and we therefore expect organizations in older, less flexible buildings to be less adaptable. Perhaps the spread of modern building techniques based on flexible use of internal wall panels will eventually eliminate this relationship.

THE FINDINGS ON ADAPTATION

All our research settings exhibited only the more improvisational forms of adaptation, which prevented testing the relative effects of improvisation.

[16] Robert Weiss, *The Process of Organization* (Ann Arbor: Institute for Social Research, The University of Michigan, 1956).

Ten Hospitals

The study of ten hospitals did not include measures of symbolic adaptation; only the two items measuring promptness and prevalence of adjustment were included. An index of these two items was constructed by the same methods used for all the other indexes discussed so far. These two were not significantly correlated with each other in the hospitals (r_S = .38), and they were related somewhat differently to the other variables. Promptness of adaptation was a function of integration and of problem-solving activities among the elite: the key members of the three major centers of power in the hospitals—the Board of Trustees, Medical Staff, and the Administrator. Authority and influence were apparently key factors in explaining the alacrity with which people changed their routines. Prevalence of adaptation was also influenced by elite characteristics, but, unlike promptness, it was facilitated by horizontal integration. Interdepartmental conflict was deleterious to adaptability, and the early efforts of authorities to alleviate it and to maintain cohesive organization were essential. Additional data showed that, when the director of nursing was considered aware of problems and effective in solving them, the hospital was more likely to be adaptive. It should be remembered that none of these elite characteristics was related to productivity.

Cultural and social-psychological factors were related differently to measures of behavioral adaptation. As expected, identification with the hospitals or parts of them were not related to adaptability. Identification can lead to resistance to change in features of the hospital that the individual wishes to preserve. Common points of view were similar to horizontal integrative factors in that they were related to prevalence but not to promptness of adaptation. This variable may be among those that facilitate development of negotiated orders. Finally, the greater the clarity of the rules, the more prevalent was adjustment. Conformity to rules requires clarity, but, more than that, clear rules introduce an element of rationality into the work environment and enable individuals to take more positive attitudes toward their organizations and requests for change.

Some of the effects of professionalism and length of service are shown in Table 3-4. Hospitals were less likely to be adaptable when they had high proportions of registered nurses on their staffs. Registered nurses were rare in these hos-

TABLE 3-3 Characteristics of Hospitals and Adaptability

CHARACTERISTICS OF HOSPITALS	PREVALENCE OF ADJUSTMENT	PROMPTNESS OF ADJUSTMENT	INDEX OF BEHAVIORAL ADAPTATION
Horizontal integration			
Extent to which related activities are well timed in everyday hospital routines	.53*	.15	.56
Extent to which people avoid creating problems for one another	.66	.29	.63
Ease of exchanging ideas about problems related to work	.55	−.03	.39
Degree to which interdepartmental problems are well handled	.54	.33	.64
Tension and conflict among key departments (summary measure)	−.53	−.55	−.72
Feelings of unreasonable pressure to perform	−.65	−.17	−.58
Vertical and elite integration			
Extent to which medical staff understands needs and problems of board of trustees	.60	.64	.79
Extent to which board of trustees understands needs and problems of medical staff	.72	.67	.87
Communication between administrator and:			
medical staff	.53	.69	.81
board of trustees	.57	.55	.55
department heads	.57	.79	.82
as assessed by these groups			
Extent to which administrator is aware of problems faced by hospital staff	.56	.61	.77
Extent to which administrator solves hospital problems effectively	.58	.78	.81
Cultural and social-psychological integration			
Identification with:			
the hospital and its goals	.45	.05	.38
one's profession	.37	.20	.17
one's work group	.11	.31	.31
Extent to which people from different departments see one another's points of view about mutual work relations	.66	.07	.56
Clarity of rules and regulations	.74	.14	.68

*Spearman rank-order correlations were used. The total sample included ten hospitals, and therefore r_s = .56, significant at the .05 level, and r_s = .75, significant at the .01 level.

pitals, however, they definitely enjoyed a seller's market. They also exhibited the higher mobility associated with the middle classes in general. When they did not like particular hospitals, they could leave and find other jobs easily. Also many older nurses were likely to be defensive about their nursing techniques. They had been taught the "right" way to do things, and they often clung to it as a defense against younger nurses who had learned a newer "right" way. Conflict with administrators also contributed to registered nurses' unwillingness to agree to changes requested by the latter: "Why should I listen to him? He hasn't any medical training; he's just a bookkeeper!"

In contrast, practical nurses were very vulnerable to change. They had had very short (usually one year or less) formal training or none at all. They were treated as second-class citizens and expected to conform to the demands of their superiors. They had no professional association to watch over their interests. Finally, they usually came from less mobile, working-class families, and, as they were usually helping to support their families, they could not easily leave to take nursing jobs in other communities.

Promptness in adaptation also declined with the length of service of the administrator. It is likely that older admin-

TABLE 3-4 Characteristics of Hospitals and Adaptability

CHARACTERISTICS OF HOSPITALS	PREVALENCE OF ADJUSTMENT	PROMPTNESS OF ADJUSTMENT	INDEX OF BEHAVIORAL ADAPTATION
Staff characteristics			
Proportion of nursing staff personnel who are registered nurses with more than five years of service	−.60*	−.58	−.65
Proportion of nursing staff personnel who are practical nurses with more than five years of service	.01	−.12	−.08
Extent by which the proportion of registered nurses exceeds that of practical nurses	−.76	−.56	−.87
Length of administrator's service	−.31	−.66	−.48
Age of the hospital building	−.70	−.66	−.88

*Spearman rank-order correlations were used. The total sample included ten hospitals, and therefore r_s = .56, significant at the .05 level, and r_s = .75, significant at the .01 level.

istrators had already done most of the innovating that they
were ever likely to do and that the rigidities of tradition had
set in. Other hospital data showed that personnel were more
likely to change promptly when they thought that past changes
had been improvements (r_s/ = .62) and when they expected numerous changes in the future (r_s = .84). Like American Presi-
dents, new hospital administrators should move early in their
tenure to make changes, and they should also make them with
sufficient frequency to maintain an ambience of change.

Older hospital buildings house less adaptive staffs. The
walls do not yield easily to new routines and technologies.
For example, knowledge that circular wards require fewer
nursing personnel is useless if one has an irrevocably rectangu-
lar building. Older buildings also tend to be staffed by nurses
and administrators with longer service (r_s = .62 and .33 respectively); the effects of this dimension have already been
noted.

Federal Agency Data

Table 3-5 provides additional data to test relationships described. All our hypotheses were confirmed by these data.
Formal coordination, levels of skill, and conditions conducive
to negotiating orders were all related to adaptability. The
rationality of the environment and the rational-trust status
of intermediate leaders were also important.

The State Department data included only one item from
the adaptability index: promptness of adjustment. It was significantly related to the adequacy of formal coordination (r =
.48, $p < .01$) and negatively related to conflict with respon-
dent's supervisor (r |= −.41). The H.E.W. study included a
measure of the extent to which each worker could depend upon
others with whom he shared a division of labor. This item was
highly correlated with the index of adaptability (r = .49,
$p < .01$).

Finally, when the degree of task structure was controlled
in the NASA-1 data, no significant differences in correlations
between adaptability and various measures of organizational
integration were obtained across the different levels of task
structure. Even if a task was fairly structured, the degree of
integration of the work group was a key independent variable
when adaptation was required.

TABLE 3-5 Organizational Characteristics and Adaptability

MEASURES OF ORGANIZATIONAL CHARACTERISTICS	INDEX OF ADAPTABILITY		
	NASA-1	NASA-2	ALPHA AGENCY
Clarity of normative environment			
Clarity of objectives toward which to work	.33*	.44	.33
Clarity of rules, policies, and guidelines	.34	†	.25
Extent to which workers are given conflicting priorities		−.21	−.11
Extent to which front office changes policies without advance notice	−.37		
Intertask structure (coordination)			
How well related jobs are meshed to achieve objectives	.59	.57	.42
Extent to which independent assignments are well planned	.51		
Conditions for negotiating orders			
Ease of exchanging ideas and information with others doing related work	.44	.51	.39
Extent to which people doing related work avoid creating problems for one another	.40	.51	.44
How well coordination problems with others doing related work are handled	.58	.60	.46
Levels of skills			
Proportion of personnel competent to do the division's work	.48		.37
Rational-trust relationship			
Extent to which front office is perceived as following its own rules	.39		
Extent to which front office is perceived as understanding workers' needs, problems, and points of view	.44		
Extent to which top management is perceived as fair and reasonable	.37		.15

*Pearson product-moment correlations were used. $N > 375$ in all cases; $r = .10$, $p < .05$; $r = .13$, $p < .01$.

†When no correlation coefficient appears, the variable was not included in that particular study.

Byberry-1

The Byberry-1 study further buttressed our findings. The adaptability index was related to

1. Clarity of objectives of work ($r = .50$)[17]
2. Clarity with which duties were defined ($r = .54$)
3. Clarity of policies and procedures ($r = .41$)

[17] All these correlations were significant beyond the .01 level.

4. Extent to which interdependent activities were well timed ($r = .38$)
5. Ease of exchanging ideas and information about mutual problems ($r = .63$)
6. Supervisor's effectiveness at solving problems ($r = .63$)
7. Supervisor's ability to use different points of view in solving problems ($r = .52$)
8. Effectiveness of director's office in solving problems ($r = .31$).

Summary of Findings on Adaptability

Adaptability varied, as did productivity, in the degree to which it was structured. But, in contrast to that for productivity, this variation in structure has very little effect on our hypotheses; it is not necessary to propose two different sets of hypotheses for high and low task structures. The reason is that, even in the most programmed situations that we studied, some significant improvisation was required. Integration at the cultural, organizational, and social-psychological levels was therefore required to facilitate communication generally and problem solving in particular. Integration of the elite in hospitals promoted both aspects of behavioral adaptation, whereas horizontal integration facilitated only the prevalence of adjustment. A high proportion of professionals among personnel was negatively related to behavioral adaptation, particularly when the professionals had long service. Older hospital buildings generally housed less adaptable staffs.

Finally, the role of management in organizations has been clarified somewhat: It is adaptive. Management must solve major problems and make major changes in routine because it alone has the authority and resources to do so. It must also maintain internal integration and conditions for developing negotiated orders. Much of the social-science literature on management has concluded that management should be primarily concerned with meeting the needs of the people who work for them. But our data suggest that a more important responsibility should be to increase effectiveness by creating and maintaining situations in which people can work. The obligation to do so is often overlooked. Perhaps the most "people-oriented" step that a manager can take is to create the kind of work environment in which our independent variables would be high: integrated, rational, and the like. Certainly the result would be greater productivity and adaptability.

HYPOTHESES ABOUT FLEXIBLE ORGANIZATIONS

Flexibility, too, can vary from highly programmed to completely improvised. Fire drills in public schools, training of public-safety officers, and planning and drilling for military contingencies are examples of programmed responses to emergencies, to temporally unpredictable overloads of work. The feature of programmed flexibility that distinguishes it from other forms is systematic inclusion of contingencies in role or job descriptions: "Under ordinary circumstances you will perform the following set of activities, but if X occurs you will perform the following set of activities...." As with production and adaptation, a comprehensive plan exists, and programmed coordination is used to implement it.

At the other end of the continuum no programs exist; each emergency is treated as a novel experience in which improvisation is the key ingredient. The hospitals in this study exhibited this form of flexibility. Because they were of medium size (100-350 beds) resident medical staffs were rare. When an emergency occurred after the day shift, it was the nursing staff that organized the initial response to it. Most such incidents mentioned in our interviews had occurred in the early morning hours and had usually involved multiple automobile accidents. Asphyxiation and burning were the next most frequent sources of emergencies. According to our respondents more than half the personnel involved in emergency treatments did some jobs that were not ordinarily theirs: registered nurses made preliminary diagnoses, practical nurses treated injuries, and aides gave medication. Had these people refused to overstep the legal boundaries of their roles, the patients might have been far worse off. Temporary role modification is a characteristic response to temporally unpredictable emergencies.

Flexibility thus differs from adaptation, in which modification of routines is intended to be more permanent. A typical emergency was described to us by a respondent; a summary may help to clarify the data that follow. Seven victims from a two-car collision were admitted to the hospital, and two of them died soon after. Only one registered nurse had originally been on duty in the emergency room. The night supervisor sent a few registered nurses, several aides, an orderly, and a student nurse to help. All the injured needed some surgery, major and minor, and the resident medical staff performed some of these operations under the direction of one surgeon. Cooperation, teamwork, and interpersonal stress were reported to have been high, but the last was disregarded by virtually everyone during and after the emergency because it was considered normal in this situation.

Between the programmed and the improvised types of flexibility are many types that combine elements of both in varying degrees. The rest of our research settings fit into this group. Ordinarily the emergencies did not consist of unusual kinds of work, as in the hospitals; rather they consisted of temporally unpredictable *overloads* of the usual work of the unit. For instance, the printing shop in one agency was instructed without prior warning to print a large quantity of a major report to Congress, using multicolor illustrations. The job was to be completed in two weeks. Although printing was obviously the normal business of this shop, this new assignment had to be meshed with the normal work load, some or all of which had to be set aside. Similar examples could be given for virtually every government division included in this study. These incidents occurred with sufficient frequency and involved such familiar tasks, however, that responses to them involved much less improvisation than was required in the hospitals. Most improvisation involved interaction with other units to reach agreement on priorities, to obtain resources (additional workers, overtime), and to ask for advice and ideas.

We expected that the organizational characteristics that facilitated each of these types of flexibility would be different in significant ways. After reviewing the "disaster" literature extant in the late 1950s, N. Demerath summarized concisely the characteristics of organizations that exhibited programmed flexibility: "Organized response to disaster situations is the more effective as solidarity is higher, plans of actions are rehearsed, roles are well-defined, plans and roles are sufficiently flexible to cope with the unexpected and the unpredictable."[18] Subsequent studies have supported this general conclusion.[19]

---

[18] N. Demerath, "Some General Propositions, An Interpretive Summary," *Human Organization* 16 (1957): 29.

[19] For an excellent summary of the literature, see C. E. Fritz, *An Inventory of Field Studies on Human Behavior in Disasters* (Washington, D.C.: Disaster Research Group, National Academy of Sciences-National Research Council, 1959).

Programmed flexibility is most satisfactory when there is a comprehensive plan of coordination, including contingent programs for emergencies; when these contingent programs are flexible enough to permit adjustment of behavior to cope with the unexpected; when the members are drilled in execution of the contingent programs; and when conditions for negotiating orders exist, so that improvised solutions to unanticipated contingencies can be devised rapidly.

When such comprehensive plans do not exist but the emergency is a temporally unpredictable overload of the usual work, some improvisation is required. Organizations that respond well to these situations have an additional set of characteristics. First, they have relatively effective routines for day-to-day production, which can be used to handle work overloads. Those with less adequate production routines experience their usual problems in extreme forms during the stress of emergencies. Second, there is sufficient personnel slack for an emergency. Third, a high proportion of professionals with long service is available. H. Wilensky found that labor-union professionals, who were often less open to adaptation, were likely to cooperate fully in emergency situations. [20] The professional with long experience is likely to have experienced similar emergencies in the past; he can facilitate improvisation by drawing on the lessons of his experience. We did not expect that morale, loyalty, commitment to objectives and other such social-psychological integrators would be related to this form of flexibility because the generally recognized need to cope with an emergency generally overrides feelings about the organization or other people.

When no comprehensive plan exists and the emergency involves work that is in some respects unusual, the necessity for improvisation is very high. The profile of the organization that copes well with such contingencies is quite different. First, authority is decentralized near the periphery of the organization, where emergencies are most likely to have their initial impact. Lower-echelon leaders have no qualms about making the necessary decisions to cope with the emergency, for they are used to making decisions for their units without referring

[20] H. Wilensky, *Intellectuals in the Labor Unions* (New York: Free Press, 1956), pp. 275-278.

problems to higher levels. Valuable time is thus saved in the coping process. Second, formal coordination is less likely to be adequate. In the absence of contingency plans, programmed coordination impedes flexibility because people are reluctant to modify their usual roles. When roles overlap and are ambiguous—as when practical nurses usually do some of the work of registered nurses and the reverse—flexibility will be highest. Third, the higher the proportion of professional personnel with long service, the greater the flexibility will be. The reasoning here is similar to that for less improvised forms of flexibility: More experienced professionals with adequate authority can draw on their experience of similar emergencies in the past to hasten the reorganization of centers of power to cope with the current emergency. In summary, then, we expect this type of flexibility in segmented organizations where authority is concomitantly decentralized and where production and adaptation are low or no more than moderate.

FINDINGS ON FLEXIBILITY

Ten Hospitals

The ten Michigan hospitals studied exhibited considerable improvisational flexibility. There were no plans for emergencies, except for atomic attacks for which plans were required by law. Table 3-6 shows how flexibility was related to the same hospital characteristics listed in Table 3-3.

The pattern that appears in Table 3-6 was strengthened by our finding that behavioral adaptation was less likely in flexible hospitals (r_s = −.43 and −.57 for prevalence and promptness of adaptation respectively). Flexibility was generally unrelated to rational and integrative organizational characteristics, but there was a strong tendency toward negative relationships for many items. Our hypothesis that flexibility is greatest in hospitals where the elite specifically and the organization generally are segmented was not clearly supported. There was a slight positive association between high levels of conflict among nursing departments and flexibility (r_s = .42). No test of our hypothesis about decentralization of authority could be made from these data.

Table 3-6 shows that experience is the best predictor of flexibility. Experienced registered nurses, who have handled

TABLE 3-6 *Characteristics of Hospitals and Flexibility*

CHARACTERISTICS OF HOSPITALS	FLEXIBILITY
Horizontal integration	
Extent to which related activities are well timed in everyday hospital routines	.20*
Extent to which people avoid creating problems for one another	—.49
Ease in exchanging ideas about problems related to work	—.04
Degree to which interdepartmental problems are well handled	.14
Tension and conflict among key departments (summary measure)	—.11
Feelings of unreasonable pressure to perform	.05
Vertical and elite integration	
Extent to which medical staff understands needs and problems of board of trustees	—.25
Extent to which board of trustees understands needs and problems of medical staff	—.39
Communication between administrator and:	
medical staff	—.21
board of trustees	—.54
department heads	—.39
as assessed by these groups	
Extent to which administrator is aware of problems faced by hospital staff	—.22
Extent to which administrator solves hospital problems effectively	—.16
Cultural and social-psychological integration	
Identification with:	
the hospital and its goals	.03
one's profession	—.02
one's work group	—.16
Extent to which people from different departments see one another's points of view about mutual work relations	—.37
Clarity of rules and regulations	—.35
Staff characteristics	
Proportion of nursing staff personnel who are registered nurses with more than five years of service	.70
Proportion of nursing staff personnel who are practical nurses with more than five years of service	.24
Extent by which the proportion of registered nurses exceeds that of practical nurses	.43
Length of administrator's service	.42
Age of the hospital building	.47

*Spearman rank-order correlations were used. The total sample included ten hospitals, and therefore $r_s = .56$, significant at the .05 level, and $r_s = .75$, significant at the .01 level.

earlier emergencies, improvise as necessary to handle current ones. Because of high turnover among registered nurses in these hospitals, most nurses with five or more years of service in any one hospital were undoubtedly in supervisory positions. The combination of authority and experience facilitated rapid improvisation in unstructured situations. There is some evidence that role overlapping was also helpful. We asked a series of questions about the extent to which people in different nursing occupational categories did one another's work (for example, to what extent registered nurses did the work of practical nurses). These items were combined with an index of role overlapping, which was correlated with flexibility (r_S = .46, $p <$ .10).

Federal Agency Data

Emergencies in the Federal agencies studied here involved temporally unpredictable overloads of accustomed work, which severely taxed the ability of the organizations to comply with imposed deadlines. As we have suggested, unpredictable work overloads were very common in these agencies, and little could be done to prepare for them because the demands of each were so different from those of others. Table 3-7 shows how flexibility was related to the organizational characteristics discussed earlier. Flexibility was related to formal coordination, levels of skill, and conditions fostering negotiated orders. In NASA and Alpha Agency flexibility was highest in those divisions that had the highest productivity (in strong contrast to our hospital findings); these units had the most workable procedures and the most competent people. Usually they could handle overloads of work well because of their procedures and because they kept sufficiently abreast of their regular work to permit their turning attention from it to handle emergencies. The value of negotiated orders is also demonstrated in Table 3-7. Help, resources, and advice from people in other units was often necessary to cope with emergencies, and interpersonal relations could reduce barriers to achieving such temporary negotiated orders.

Clarity of the normative environment contributed little to flexibility. As norms apply almost exclusively to productivity and adaptability, it is not surprising that no relationship with flexibilty was found. The only normative guideline for emergencies in the agencies studied here was "Do it, do it well, and do your regular work too."

TABLE 3-7 Organizational Characteristics and Flexibility

MEASURES OF ORGANIZATIONAL CHARACTERISTICS	MEASURE OF FLEXIBILITY		
	NASA-1	NASA-2	ALPHA AGENCY
Clarity of normative environment			
Clarity of objectives toward which to work	.24*	.29	.11
Clarity of rules, policies, and guidelines	.12	†	.12
Extent to which workers are given conflicting priorities		−.10	−.13
Extent to which front office changes policies without advance notice	−.18		
Intertask structure (coordination)			
How well related jobs are meshed to achieve objectives	.51	.43	.18
Extent to which independent assignments are well planned	.40		
Conditions for negotiating orders			
Ease of exchanging ideas and information with others doing related work	.40	.35	.27
Extent to which people doing work avoid creating problems for one another	.34	.33	.37
How well coordination problems with others doing related work are handled	.47	.44	.24
Levels of skills			
Proportion of personnel competent to do the division's work	.31		.25
Rational-trust relationship			
Extent to which front office is perceived as following its own rules	.21		
Extent to which front office is perceived as understanding workers' needs, problems, and points of view	.15		
Extent to which top management is perceived as fair and reasonable	.18		.17

*Pearson product-moment correlations were used. $N > 375$ in all cases; $r = .10$, $p < .05$; $r = .13$, $p < .01$.

†When no correlation coefficient appears, the variable was not included in that particular study.

The Byberry Data

In the Byberry hospital emergencies had a very different character; they were seldom imposed by the external environment, as in the ten hospitals already discussed. The most common type involved patients becoming uncontrollable. Little organizational mobilization was required to cope with this situation; usually one to three attendants could handle it. The next most common problem was fire; patients had to be evacuated from the threatened building, which was not easy in many buildings. Plans for such contingencies existed and were rehearsed seriously by each building staff because this type of emergency was not uncommon. Consequently, our single flexibility item applied to two radically different types of situation, one requiring a fairly simple interpersonal response and the other a massive planned response. Future studies must include multiple measures of flexibility to account for these different types of responses.

Given these limitations, our findings on flexibility in Byberry-1 present an interesting contrast to those on adaptability. The effectiveness of the director's office at solving problems, the clarity of policies and procedures, and the extent to which related activities were well timed were all unrelated to flexibility. The clarity of objectives and of the definition of work roles were moderately related to flexibility (r = .27 and .35 respectively). The strongest relationship (r = .39) was with ease in exchanging of ideas and information about work-related problems, a measure of conditions for developing negotiated orders. The overall picture was thus closer to that of the ten hospitals than to that of the government agencies.

Summary of Findings on Flexibility

None of the sites in this study exhibited programmed flexibility; our hypothesis about this type of response could not therefore be tested. The ten Michigan hospitals exhibited unstructured flexibility; those that coped well were not particularly well run, nor were they usually the ones that gave the best patient care. They were older organizations with larger cadres of experienced nurses whose professional acumen facilitated coping with emergencies. There is some slight evidence that flexible hospitals may be more segmented. This question deserves further study with more sensitive measures than those that we used. A test of our decentralization hypothesis is also necessary.

The Federal agencies revealed quite a different pattern because the nature of work overloads was similar to that of the work done every day. In these agencies the flexible divisions were also the productive ones. They performed better on a day-to-day basis. Their flexibility was not, however, related to the clarity of objectives, policies, and rules that applied to their work.

CONCLUSIONS

We can summarize our findings by showing how the independent variables discussed in this chapter were related to the overall index of organizational effectiveness. These relationships are shown in Table 3-8.

Certain aspects of the normative environment like clarity of objectives, rules, policies, and guidelines were clearly related to overall effectiveness. Assignment of conflicting priorities for different tasks appears to have been more harmful at Byberry than in the government agencies studied. These overall relationships mask some important variations noted earlier in the chapter, however. For example, there was no necessary relationship between clarity of work objectives and productivity when tasks were highly structured. The technologies and formal norms applied in structured situations were obvious representations of objectives. The clarity of the normative environment had little to do with the degree of organizational flexibility, but was very important in adaptability and in the less structured types of productivity in which cycles of improvisation were combined with productive activities.

Clarity of norms was helpful for two basic reasons. First, it created an ambience characterized by some certainty and rationality, a pleasant atmosphere that could enhance the morale of workers and increase their willingness to solve adaptive problems. In the NASA-1 study the correlation between clarity of objectives and the extent to which respondents reported that their fellow workers were trying hard to do a good job was $r = .38$. Clarity of objectives was also highly correlated with job satisfaction ($r = .45$). Second, the normative environment could facilitate solution of adaptive problems by providing a set of values or priorities that could be used in decision-making. We use the term "could" because it is essential to avoid the functionalist assumption of automatic adjustment: that people tend to adjust to the social values of the collectivities in which they live or work. In the truly adaptive organization personnel will often consider alternative values and norms as guides to their decisions.

There was also a strong relationship between functional integration and effectiveness. Such intergration was achieved through a combination of formal norms and negotiated orders. Highly structured tasks reflected the application of formal

TABLE 3-8 Organizational Characteristics and Overall Effectiveness

MEASURES OF ORGANIZATIONAL CHARACTERISTICS	INDEX OF OVERALL EFFECTIVENESS			
	NASA-1	NASA-2	ALPHA AGENCY	BYBERRY-1*
Clarity of normative environment				
Clarity of objectives toward which to work	.19†	.46	.36	.48
Clarity of rules, policies, and guidelines	.24	§	.27	.33
Extent to which workers are given conflicting priorities		−.12	−.03	−.34
Extent to which front office changes policies without advance notice	−.34			
Intertask structure (coordination)				
How well related jobs are meshed to achieve objectives	.59	.58	.43	.35
Extent to which independent assignments are well planned	.44			
Conditions for negotiating orders				
Ease of exchanging ideas and information with others doing related work	.32	.48	.37	.56
Extent to which people doing related work avoid creating problems for one another	.35	.40	.35	
How well coordination problems with others doing related work are handled	.51	.59	.47	
Levels of skills				
Proportion of personnel competent to do the division's work	.43		.35	
Rational-trust relationship				
Extent to which front office is perceived as following its own rules	.33			
Extent to which front office is perceived as understanding workers' needs, problems, and points of view	.37			
Extent to which top management is perceived as fair and reasonable	.34		.15	

*Includes only those respondents directly involved in treating patients.

†Pearson product-moment correlations were used. $N > 375$ in all cases except Byberry-1 in which $N > 130$. For $N = 130$, $r = .17$, $P < .05$; $r = .23$, $p < .01$. For $N = 375$, $r = .10$, $p < .05$; $r = .13$, $p < .01$.

§When no correlation coefficient appears, the variable was not included in that particular study.

norms, and effectiveness was then a function of the adequacy of the coordinating plan and the levels of skills among the personnel who implemented it. Conditions for negotiating orders contributed to all forms of effectiveness but least when productive tasks were highly structured.

The role of management in achieving organizational effectiveness has been somewhat clarified by our studies. Managerial involvement was often essential to the solution of major adaptive problems. Furthermore, management could bind the organization both vertically and horizontally, creating the setting in which general adaptability was most likely to occur. To accomplish such integration, managers had to solve problems of coordination to prevent organizational segmentation and to create new integrative linkages when needed between people and groups. When rational-trust characteristics were associated with management, the organization was likely to be more effective (see Table 3-8). Finally, in our study of ten hospitals, promptness of adjustment to change was shown to be a function of the integration of the three elites that led each hospital, but prevalence of adjustment was primarily a function of general organizational integration. Similar findings occurred in the Byberry studies. By definition, integrated elites concentrate power and reduce vertical organizational barriers; there are fewer places for the potential deviant to hide, and probably too much power backs elite decisions for him to be able to resist them.

Perhaps our most provocative finding involved flexibility. When flexibility resulted from careful planning for contingencies or involved usual kinds of work in unusual amounts, the characteristics of flexible organizations were similar to those of adaptive organizations. But, when flexibility involved completely improvised responses to emergencies, the most flexible organizations appeared to be slightly segmented; clarity of roles was low as were productivity and adaptability. These findings must be interpreted with caution. Our flexibility measure included only a single item; more sensitive measures are required to determine the precise amounts of improvisation required by different types of emergencies.

4
Decision-Making
and
Effectiveness

In Chapter 1 we defined and discussed the concepts of social power, authority, and influence. In this chapter we shall pursue several interrelated objectives; underlying all of them is an analysis of how decision-making is structured in different organizations and the consequences of these different configurations for effectiveness and other aspects of group life. First, we shall examine the notions of "structures" of power, authority, and decision-making. Are they the same or different? If they are different, how are they related to one another? Second, using our answers to these questions, we shall focus on the relationship between each of several decision-making structures and organizational effectiveness. Third, we shall analyze the effects of varying degrees of integration among decision-making elites on organizational effectiveness. Fourth, we shall investigate the impact of configurations of decision-making on other aspects of group life. Finally, we shall discuss the effects of varying degrees of legitimacy in decision-making structures on effectiveness and on some social-psychological dimensions of organizational behavior.

CONFIGURATIONS OF POWER, AUTHORITY, AND DECISION-MAKING

In Chapter 1 we noted that organizations can be viewed as collections of centers of power whose interrelations are to some degree structured at their interfaces. We can therefore imagine structures, or configurations, of relationships among these centers of power. We can also imagine similar configurations of authority. There are two major dimensions along which configurations of power and authority vary: centralization and social

integration. As the integration of centers of power and its relationship to organizational effectiveness was discussed in Chapter 2, we shall concentrate on centralization here. Later in this
chapter we shall combine the notions of social power and integration in an investigation of the impact of integration of elites
on organizational effectiveness.

Power and authority in human groups can be measured
on a continuum ranging from complete centralization in a
single subgroup or role to total and equal decentralization
among all subgroups or roles. It is theoretically convenient to
identify five points along this continuum: centralized, fairly
centralized, balanced, fairly decentralized, and decentralized.[1]
(In discussing the characteristics of organizations with these
varying degrees of centralization of power and authority we
shall focus only on authority structures, for identical comments
apply to power configurations.)

In a centralized authority structure all authority is lodged
in a single subgroup or individual in the organization. There
are two significant types of roles: elite and non-elite. Communication patterns are simple: lateral communication is discouraged except on functionally relevant matters, information but
not advice is sent upward, orders but not requests for advice
are sent downward. Overt behavior conforms to perceived
elite values. The elite usually fosters competition for rewards
among the non-elite, in order to keep the latter internally divided. Members of the non-elite therefore become very circum-
spect about expressing their private attitudes in front of one
another and before the elite.

In the fairly centralized configuration of authority spe-
cialization and subgroup formation are encouraged or expected.
These developments, however, serve to decentralize authority
somewhat and to change the nature of intergroup communication. Lateral communication is abundant and difficult for
the elite to control. Suggestions, recommendations, and advice
are sent to the elite, which uses cadres of advisors. Much information flows upward, though some that reflects poorly on
the performance of the non-elites is blocked before it reaches
the elite. The elite reserves to itself final decisions on major
matters. Overt value consensus is relatively high but not as
high as in a centralized organization.

[1] Guy E. Swanson, *Religion and Regime: A Sociological Account of the
Reformation* (Ann Arbor: The University of Michigan Press, 1967).

In the Office of Administration at the National Aeronautics and Space Administration this configuration of authority was standard. In fact, reality conformed to this Weberian ideal to an almost incredible degree; on a control graph[2] of the office and its divisions and branches a straight line sloped downward from the point of greatest influence (top management in the office), corresponding exactly with the formally allocated authority of each succeeding office.

At the balanced midpoint on the centralization continuum one subgroup or role has, over an extended period of time, access to the same amount of authority as do all the other subgroups or roles combined. This unit must therefore be a party to every dominating coalition, and the interests of this major unit are likely to shape those of some other units considerably. In contrast to the situation in the more centralized configurations, members of the minor units have greater opportunities to pursue their self-interests.

In fairly decentralized organizations authority is so diffuse that no subgroup or role can order the others. The units do not have equal or nearly equal authority; one unit may have several times as much as another has but not enough to dominate the latter. These subgroups represent their special interests, and collective action requires some peaceful means of resolving conflict among the subgroups and of deciding how to act collectively. The politics of bargaining and coalition formation is common and the milieu of such politics is committees, parliaments, informal meetings, and so forth. Consensus on values is usually minimal, reflecting the special orientations of the units. The ten medium-sized hospitals in our study conformed to this pattern; the units usually included boards of trustees, administrators, key medical personnel, and some department heads.

In extreme decentralization all subgroups or roles have equal authority. Groups of this type are becoming increasingly common in federally decentralized organizations, in which most functional specialists have counterparts with equal amounts of authority in each of the other units in the organization. In order to create a new policy, for example, on travel regulations, it is often necessary for the directors of financial management from all the field centers to meet and agree. Groups of

[2] Arnold S. Tannenbaum, "Control and Effectiveness in a Voluntary Organization," *American Journal of Sociology* 67 (1961): 33-46.

specialists designing future automobiles or attacking a problem in chemical synthesis often have decentralized authority structures. Likert-style management groups also approximate this configuration, though Rensis Likert does not consider them decentralized only in terms of authority; he favors decentralization of power and decision-making as well.

DECISION-MAKING STRUCTURES

So far we have said nothing about decision-making structures and their relations to power and authority configurations. The prototype of this concept emerged from studies of community elites.[3] A strategy that involved sampling the universe of issues being discussed in a community was designed. The researcher could then trace who was involved in making (or failing to make) decisions on each issue and how the decision-makers were related to one another in this process. The resulting sociometric "structure" would reveal who were the most influential and least influential people and how they were organized in relation to one another. This method has been used to identify decision-making elites in a wide variety of studies.[4] Such structures can be rigid or amorphous, permanent or ephemeral, complete or with significant gaps. Certainly they can vary in degree of centralization.

What are the relationships among power, authority, and decision-making structures? The configurations of power and authority even in formal organizations are not necessarily congruent, primarily because power has several other bases beside legitimate authorization: expertise, resources, friendship, and so on. In addition, human beings do not always design their authority systems to match their power configurations; strong city-manager forms of government are often adopted in communities with decentralized power structures. NASA had a hierarchical authority system, but power was decentralized among the field centers to a degree greater than the structure

[3] For a more detailed discussion of this technique, see Paul E. Mott, "Configurations of Power," in *The Structure of Community Power*, ed. Michael Aiken and Mott (New York: Random House, 1970), pp. 85-100.

[4] See, for example, Stephen K. Bailey, *Congress Makes a Law: The Story Behind the Employment Act of 1946* (New York: Columbia University Press, 1950); M. K. Jennings, *Community Influentials: The Elites of Atlanta* (New York: Free Press, 1964); Richard C. Snyder, H. W. Bruck, and Burton Sapin, eds., *Foreign Policy Decision-Making: An Approach to the Study of International Politics* (New York: Free Press, 1962).

of authority would have indicated. In all the ten Michigan hospitals studied the highest authority was vested in the boards of trustees, but the greatest access to power was variously located in each hospital: in the boards, offices of the administrators, medical personnel, or, more likely, some combination of the three. When the configurations of power and authority are congruent, that is, when both are centralized or fairly centralized, then the decision-making structures are likely to be congruent also for there are few, if any, significant bases remaining for their development. For example, when both power and authority are fairly decentralized, the decision-making structure is likely to be parliamentary, and decision processes will include bargaining and formation of coalitions.

When power and authority configurations are not congruent, however, some interesting variations in decision-making structures appear. The federally decentralized organizational model that is frequently used in industrial organizations generates centralized power and decentralized authority. The decision-making process has two stages: Power holders make general policy and set parameters within which lower-echelon personnel are free to make decisions (to negotiate orders).

None of the macrostructures within which our study units were located exhibited this type of incongruence; fairly centralized authority and fairly decentralized power were more common. In these organizations the authority structures prescribed that final decisions should be made by the highest officials, on the basis of staff recommendations, and orders given to lower-level personnel. But, as significant power resided elsewhere, these orders could often be resisted effectively. Consequently, the decision-making structures were parliamentary but replete with nuances designed to maintain the illusion of managerial authority. For example, at NASA, policy decisions proposed by headquarters were usually circulated among the field centers for "comment." Significant objections from the field centers to a "proposed policy issuance" usually resulted in "reevaluation" of the proposal. Major policy decisions were usually made by groups of center directors or their representatives and headquarters personnel.

This parliamentary structure of decision-making was also prevalent among the other organizations included in this study. Each of the ten Michigan hospitals had decision-making structures involving some combination of people from each of the different elite groups. These coalitions varied in their composition and stability, depending upon the issues, maintenance of friendships, common interests (including avocations), and even changes in physical location. In Alpha Agency the authority system had to be sufficiently flexible to facilitate the grouping of specialists from different units to work on specific problems. In all our studies of Federal agencies, which extend well beyond those discussed here, we have yet to find one whose macrostructure comes close to Weber's concept of the ideal bureaucracy. All were highly open systems that could not be understood unless their interfaces with Congress, private interest groups, and other bureaucracies were taken into account. At the level of divisions within these agencies, however, a different picture emerged: The combination of centralized authority and decentralized power rarely existed because there were few viable bases of power other than authority. Power and authority were lodged fairly congruently in roles, and the prescribed authority systems were fairly centralized. The structure of decision-making was primarily a function of the division directors' preferences in management styles and of their personalities. As the data presented here will show, most division directors were perceived as using the prescribed, fairly centralized structure, but some preferred other structures or used different arrangements with different people. To measure how major decisions were made, we asked the following question of all personnel in the NASA-2, Alpha Agency, and Byberry studies:

> Which of the following ways comes closest to describing how *the important decisions* are made in your division or office?
>
> _____(1) The division chief or office head makes the important decisions. He rarely asks for advice; he just gives orders.
>
> _____(2) The division chief or office head makes the *final* decisions, but he relies on other people in the division or office for advice and recommendations.
>
> _____(3) Some important decisions are made by the division chief or office head; but about as many are made by other people in the division or office.

_____(4) Several different people make the important decisions. The division chief or office head *really* doesn't have much more influence then any of them.

_____(5) A number of people are about equally involved. They usually get together and discuss the problem and agree on a solution.

_____(8) I don't know how the important decisions are made in my division or office.

The distribution of responses and mean scores on this item among the divisions in the Federal agencies where it was administered are shown in Table 4-1. Two observations can readily be made from the data in this table. First, the vast majority of respondents in both agencies regarded their divisions as having fairly centralized decision-making structures. Second, there were nevertheless appreciable numbers who disagreed with this modal assessment, and in some divisions the disagreements varied considerably from one another. These variations were functions of position, perception, and division directors' different styles of decision-making for different people and issues. Even the responses of supervisors, those closest to the division directors, reflected no greater agreement than that reflected in the general figures shown in Table 4-1.

During our two and a half years at NASA, Divisions A and

TABLE 4-1 Distributions of Responses to Decision-Making Question in NASA-2 and Alpha Agency

NASA-2 DIVISION CODE	FREQUENCY DISTRIBUTIONS OF RESPONSES					ALPHA AGENCY DIVISION CODE	FREQUENCY DISTRIBUTIONS OF RESPONSES				
	CENTRAL-IZED		◄——►	DECENTRAL-IZED			CENTRAL-IZED		◄——►	DECENTRAL-IZED	
A	2	4	1	0	1	A	1	19	1	0	1
B	0	9	0	0	0	B	2	28	3	2	0
C	1	7	2	0	1	C	2	15	0	0	2
D	0	19	2	1	3	D	0	21	2	1	1
E	1	28	3	0	0	E	2	11	0	0	0
F	3	20	5	1	3	F	1	13	2	0	1
G	1	20	0	0	0	G	0	7	8	0	0
H	20	31	10	2	7	H	5	25	7	0	2
I	0	13	0	0	0	I	2	29	2	0	1
J	3	11	2	0	2	J	0	0	4	8	4
K	3	33	0	0	3	K	0	28	8	1	1
L	12	36	26	1	3	L	1	13	2	0	0
						M	1	19	3	1	0

L seemed the most centralized, even more so than these data indicate. Both division directors made all major decisions (and many minor ones) themselves, involved themselves in the minutiae of staff projects, and maintained one-to-one relations with their subordinates while discouraging lateral communication among them. The branch chiefs complained that they were too closely monitored by their division directors and given too little opportunity to develop their own plans for their respective areas. Division H was different. The director had been appointed about one year before our study began, with a mandate to improve a division that was considered ineffective and staffed by generally mediocre branch chiefs and supervisors. His efforts were successful, but during the transition all requests from top management came directly to him, rather than to the appropriate branches. This structural factor added to the centralization of decision-making in his division.

Less can be said about the divisions in Alpha Agency because we spent only six months there. The director of Division J was a laissez-faire manager. He was very close to retirement age and preferred to leave the work of the division to his subordinates.

THE STRUCTURE OF DECISION-MAKING AND EFFECTIVENESS

Our basic hypothesis was: *There is no necessary relationship between the degree of centralization of decision-making and organizational effectiveness.* A decentralized decision-making structure imposed on an organization with a more centralized configuration of power can create havoc. The opposite is also true. To force such overlays increases the difficulty of decision-making. A series of social arrangements must evolve ad hoc to help reach a compromise between the requirements of both structures. These arrangements are, however, seldom blessed with the useful aura of legitimacy. The experience of the city-manager reform movement is instructive on this point. [5] Attempts to impose this hierarchical model on cities with decentralized power configurations have repeatedly failed, for it does not engender a milieu in which the powerful interest groups can engage in coalition formation. Sometimes the city manager is retained but becomes little more than a well-paid clerk serving a powerful city council that does reflect the in-

[5] This argument and the evidence for it are outlined in greater detail in Mott, *op. cit.*, pp. 85-100.

terests of community groups. Many people find such situations unpleasant to work in, and their effectiveness is accordingly impaired. It is rather naive to argue that the solution to this problem is always to change the configuration of power. Sometimes it can and should be changed, but often it cannot or should not be changed. Configurations of power represent responses to rather pervasive and compelling social and technological forces, often the optimal and even necessary adjustments to these forces. Do we favor decentralization of power or authority in air-traffic control, meteorological services, or refereeing football games?

The legitimacy of the decision-making structure in the eyes of those who must use it is a vital factor in its acceptance and effectiveness. Guy E. Swanson found that, when one type of decision-making structure was deemed legitimate by organizational members, their morale and effectiveness declined if they were required to use another type of structure.[6] The legitimacy of the decision-making structure is quite relative, however. A person may consider the centralized model legitimate for the organization in which he works but not for a voluntary association to which he belongs or for the city in which he lives.

Personality characteristics are also related to preference for particular configurations of decision-making. We generally assume that in this pluralistic society most people are fairly flexible and will work productively and find ways to achieve personal growth and satisfaction in a fairly broad range of decision-making configurations. Some people will not, however. W. Haythorn and Victor H. Vroom showed that workers with high authoritarianism (F-scale) scores, that is, who are rigid and intolerant of ambiguity, and who prefer structured tasks exhibited higher morale and greater productivity under authoritarian supervisors. Conversely, workers who had low F-scale scores—who were flexible, capable of coping with uncertainties, and who preferred more autonomy or self-direction—preferred more democratic supervision and exhibited low morale and productivity under authoritarian supervision.[7]

[6] Guy E. Swanson, "The Effectiveness of Decision-Making Groups," *Adult Leadership* 8 (June, 1959): 48-52.

[7] W. Haythorn, "The Effects of Varying Compositions of Authoritarian and Equalitarian Leaders and Followers," in *Readings in Social Psychology*, ed. E. Maccoby, T. Newcomb, and E. Hartley (New York: Holt, Rinehart and

As a majority of Americans tend to score toward the lower end of the F scale, it seems probable that they dislike centralized decision-making structures.

This finding cannot be generalized to all cultures, however. Furthermore, certain professions are known to attract people who need greater autonomy. Medicine is the classic example, but many professions involving creative research are attractive for the same reason. Training for these professions often involves further socialization in the virtues of autonomous decision-making. That certain occupations are more attractive to people with certain types of personality needs is well established.[8] To the extent that people have adequate information and are free to act on it, they will tend to select those occupations that serve their needs. Studies of one occupation may reflect a positive correlation between centralization of decision-making and effectiveness, whereas those of another might reveal a negative correlation. Finally, Robert Tannenbaum and Fred Massarik have concluded that the decentralized model is appropriate when there is sufficient time to use it, when members of the organization are competent to make the required decisions, when workers' commitment is desired, and when managers are willing to accept any decision that the group makes.[9] This conclusion suggests that a manager might use different styles of decision-making under different circumstances.

All these factors—congruence and legitimacy of configurations, personality factors, professional expectations, levels of competence, time, and desired outcomes—can be studied in a great many different combinations to determine which configurations of decision-making are appropriate for specific groups of people doing specific kinds of work in specific cultures. As they are all present in large organizations, we can expect no necessary relationship between effectiveness and

---

Winston, 1958), pp. 511-521; and Victor H. Vroom, "Some Personality Determinants of the Effects of Participation," *Journal of Abnormal and Social Psychology* 59 (1959): 322-327.

8 For example, see Neal C. Gross, W. S. Mason, and A. W. McEachern, *Explorations in Role Analysis: Studies of the School Superintendency Role* (New York: Wiley, 1958).

9 Robert Tannenbaum and Fred Massarik, "Participation by Subordinates in the Managerial Decision-Making Process," *The Canadian Journal of Economics and Political Science* (August 1950), pp. 408-418.

centralization of the decision-making structure. The existence of positive or negative findings—and there are plenty of both—reveals the presence of selection mechanisms that have resulted in skewed populations or highly specialized sets of functional needs, rather than telling us something about the relationship between centralization of decision-making and effectiveness.

DATA RELATING DECISION-MAKING STRUCTURES AND ORGANIZATIONAL EFFECTIVENESS

The items used to measure perceptions of the structure of decision-making and organizational effectiveness were included in the NASA-2, Alpha Agency, and Byberry studies. Table 4-2 shows the results for all respondents in the NASA-2 study. Some readers may question our inclusion of all responses in this analysis because lower-echelon personnel might not know how decisions were actually made. Two facts mitigate this criticism: First, all but two or three divisions were small enough so that the actions of the leaders were ordinarily fairly visible, and, second, respondents could answer "I don't know," as almost 100 people did. Nevertheless, the possibility of ignorance was tested by drawing up a similar table including the responses of only professionals and supervisors with G.S. 11 or higher ratings. Selection of "several people" and "group decisions" was then too small to analyze, but the overall pattern remained as in Table 4-2.

This table includes several important findings. The correlation coefficients across the bottom show no relationship between centralization of decision-making and any of our measures of effectiveness. To test the possibility that this absence may have resulted from some curvilinearity in the relationship, we controlled type of decision-making structure and obtained new mean scores of effectiveness. Then the centralized style was least associated with division effectiveness. Centralization had its most serious impact on production and on the early, symbolic stages of adaptation. The usual reason given for lower production in centralized organizations is that this model of decision-making is repugnant to the personalities and values of most Americans, particularly professional workers. Our data do show that job satisfaction was lower in the more centralized divisions, indicating low morale and little inducement to produce.

TABLE 4-2 Centralization of Decision-Making and Effectiveness, All NASA-2 Personnel

PERCEIVED LOCUS OF DECISION-MAKING	N	PRODUCTIVITY				ADAPTABILITY				INDEX OF OVERALL EFFECTIVENESS
		QUAN-TITY	QUAL-ITY	EFFI-CIENCY	KEEPING UP TO DATE	ANTICI-PATING PROBLEMS	PREV-ALENCE	PROMPT-NESS	FLEXI-BILITY	
Division director	46	3.30*	3.60	2.91	3.00	2.52	3.38	3.47	3.80	3.16
Division director with advice of subordinates	231	3.90	4.01	3.50	3.66	3.50	3.90	3.81	4.12	3.68
Division director half the time; others half the time	41	3.75	3.90	3.32	3.55	3.18	3.69	3.56	3.95	3.61
Several people	5†	3.80	3.60	3.40	3.20	3.00	3.40	3.80	3.80	3.50
Group decisions	23	3.81	3.90	3.29	3.76	3.38	3.67	3.67	4.00	3.68
F test (4/345)		4.50	3.34	4.82	5.97	10.25	2.38	1.40	1.57	8.85
Probability		.01	.05	.01	.01	.01	N.S.§	N.S.	N.S.	.01
Pearson coefficients	r =	.08	.04	.05	.12	.10	.01	.01	.01	.09
of correlation	N =	335	335	335	337	335	325	332	337	340
	p =	N.S.	N.S.	N.S.	N.S.	N.S.	N.S.	N.S.	N.S.	N.S.

*The higher the score, the higher is the measure of the variable, for example, the higher is the quantity, quality, or efficiency of production.

†Obviously there were too few instances to warrant analysis; the mean scores have nevertheless been included for the reader's inspection.

§Not significant.

We shall also propose an additional explanation, however. One of the major findings discussed in Chapter 3 was that effective managers involve themselves minimally in the production process. (The forms that even this involvement might take will be discussed in Chapter 6.) The authoritarian manager has no such restraint but he involves himself directly and intimately in the production process. The heads of the three most centralized divisions studied at NASA shared a common view of their subordinates as second-rate in talent, motivation, and performance: therefore they watched them closely and redid most of their work. One such manager evaded the latter task by the simple expedient of handling all the more complex (and most interesting) projects himself. The other two always had stacks of work on their desks, including reports from their subordinates awaiting the managerial "massage." These division directors created production bottlenecks because they could not possibly keep pace with the efforts of all their subordinates. The subordinates recognized this fact and learned to disregard the production deadlines set for them by the directors. Significantly, in the NASA-1 study these three division directors had been among the four ranked as the closest supervisors in the Office of Administration.

That centralization also results in lower estimates of others' ability to anticipate problems and to keep up with changing techniques is not surprising. It is extremely difficult to monitor this kind of performance. Furthermore, effective performance requires a significant element of voluntarism; individuals must want to keep up to date and to be sensitive to problems. There is little in the centralized structure to elicit these attitudes; the contrary result is more likely. In the U.S. State Department we asked all respondents how much team spirit there was in their divisions and how much the division directors involved them in decision-making. The less involvement permitted, the lower team spirit was ($r = .35, n = 537, p < .01$). The individual is unlikely to give more of himself than the situation requires. If he becomes aware of a new problem, he can always feign ignorance, and, if he is convincing, he can enjoy the discomfiture of his director when the problem comes to his attention. Furthermore, there is little point in keeping abreast of innovations when the director customarily takes credit for his subordinates' efforts.

But there is ample reason to adapt to changes favored by the authoritarian director, including unexpected work overloads, because failure to do so would likely incur severe negative sanctions. The distinction between overt and covert responses is thus critical to understanding why workers in centralized divisions are highly responsive to changes initiated by their bosses, but less inclined to initiate changes themselves. J. L. Price's conclusion that centralized work groups are not adaptive cannot be supported.[10] When authoritarian leaders develop specialists in identification of problems and innovation, there is no reason why their organizations cannot be as adaptive as less centralized ones are. Common adherence to a democratic value system may explain why this possibility is so often discounted.

Except for the centralized model, no decision-making structure revealed any clear superiority in enhancing organizational effectiveness. T tests among the four remaining mean scores in any column were not significant. The fairly centralized model consistently produced the highest mean scores, but to conclude that it is the best structure for effective functioning would be erroneous. In our years of work at NASA we learned that the fairly centralized model had been culturally prescribed as *the* legitimate way to organize decision-making. At Alpha Agency this prescription had been modified somewhat. One long-time employee put it this way: "If I am walking down the hall and see a meeting in progress, I ought to be able to tell what problem the group is working on by who is in the meeting." The bureaucratic structure had to be flexible enough to allow for specific groups to form to work on each problem and to engage easily in joint decision-making, regardless of differences in the authority of the members. This philosophy is reflected in Table 4-3. The fairly centralized structure did not even *tend* to reveal superiority in effective functioning over the balanced configuration. Other than this trivial effect of legitimacy the pattern in Table 4-3 is remarkably similar to that in Table 4-2. First, the centralized model was the least effective in production and the initial phases of adaptation. Second, it was equally effective in behavioral adaptation and

10 J. L. Price, *Organizational Effectiveness: A Propositional Inventory* (Homewood, Ill.: Irwin, 1968), pp. 79-80.

TABLE 4-3 *Centralization of Decision-Making and Effectiveness, All Alpha Agency Respondents*

PERCEIVED LOCUS OF DECISION-MAKING	N	PRODUCTIVITY			ADAPTABILITY					INDEX OF OVERALL EFFECTIVENESS
		QUAN-TITY	QUAL-ITY	EFFI-CIENCY	KEEPING UP TO DATE	ANTICI-PATING PROBLEMS	PREV-ALENCE	PROMPT-NESS	FLEXI-BILITY	
Division director	20	3.70*	3.80	2.90	3.33	2.80	4.22	3.56	4.30	3.44
Division director, with advice of subordinates	259	4.36	4.20	3.49	3.69	3.39	4.22	4.06	4.51	3.91
Division director half the time, others half the time	47	4.37	4.13	3.50	3.46	3.39	4.37	4.08	4.55	3.96
Several people	15	4.00	4.00	3.08	3.54	3.15	3.69	3.69	4.31	3.69
Group decisions	19	4.20	4.40	3.00	3.60	3.00	4.20	3.60	3.80	3.73
F test (4/360)		4.01	3.42	2.68	3.28	3.24	1.84	2.01	3.41	6.45
Probability		.01	.01	.05	.05	.05	N.S.†	N.S.	.01	.01
Pearson coefficients of correlation	$r =$	−.06	−.06	.00	.01	−.03	−.01	−.01	.00	
	$N =$	352	352	349	345	348	343	345	352	
	$p =$	N.S.	N.S.	N.S.	N.S.	N.S.	N.S.	N.S	N.S.	

*The higher the score, the higher is the measure of the variable, for example, the higher is the quantity, quality, or efficiency of production.

†Not significant.

flexibility. Third, the other four configurations were essentially equal in facilitating effective functioning.[11]

The Byberry-1 findings conformed, with one exception, to those from the other sites. The major difference was that behavioral adaptation at Byberry was significantly lower when decisions were perceived as being made centrally. This finding introduces an interesting consideration. Unlike the NASA or Alpha Agency division directors Byberry department heads were often quite distant physically from many of the people whom they supervised, especially the ward attendants. The wards were often two or three floors away from the supervisors' offices. The registered nurses' work brought them into more frequent contact with the nursing supervisor for the building. To test this explanation, we compared the responses of registered nurses, practical nurses, and attendants, to questions about whether or not decision-making in their units was highly centralized and on the promptness of their adjustment to changes (see Table 4-4). The responses were clearly related to position: All but one of the attendants said that they responded to changes very slowly, whereas all registered nurses said that they responded fairly rapidly. The one attendant who said that she responded to change very quickly was also the only attendant who mentioned a preference for centralized decision-making.

INTEGRATION OF THE ELITES AND EFFECTIVENESS

As no measures of integration of the elites were taken in our studies of government agencies, it is impossible to examine relationships between this characteristic and effectiveness at

---

[11] Yet another way to illustrate our basic finding is the following table from the NASA-2 study.

DIVISION EFFECTIVENESS AND CENTRALIZATION OF DECISION-MAKING

RATING OF OVERALL DIVISION EFFECTIVENESS	PERCEPTION OF WHO MADE IMPORTANT DECISIONS*	N
Poor	4.53	17
Fair	3.90	51
Good	3.62	79
Very good	3.75	134
Excellent	3.83	54

*On this scale 5.00 = centralized decision structure, and 1.00 = decentralized decision structure; $F(4/335) = 3.84$; probability = .05.

TABLE 4-4 Centralization of Decision-Making and Effectiveness, All Byberry-1 Respondents

PERCEIVED LOCUS OF DECISION-MAKING	N	PRODUCTIVITY				ADAPTABILITY				INDEX OF OVERALL EFFECTIVENESS
		QUAN-TITY	QUAL-ITY	EFFI-CIENCY	KEEPING UP TO DATE	ANTICI-PATING PROBLEMS	PREV-ALENCE	PROMPT-NESS	FLEXI-BILITY	
Department heads	16	3.50	3.44	2.69	2.25	2.62	2.31	2.06	3.93	2.85
Department heads, with advice of subordinates	146	4.25	4.08	3.63	3.78	3.84	4.26	3.69	4.20	3.98
Department heads half the time, others half the time	11	4.40	3.82	3.45	3.40	3.36	3.55	3.09	4.00	3.71
Several people	2	-	-	-	-	-	-	-	-	-
Group decisions	23	4.30	4.00	3.52	3.77	3.38	4.36	3.59	3.95	3.88
F test (4/200)		6.05	3.62	5.28	10.58	7.57	10.19	6.43	1.28	13.11
Probability		.01	.01	.01	.01	.01	.01	.01	N.S.§	.01
Pearson coefficients of correlation	$r =$	−.15	.00	.00	−.06	.10	−.11	−.07	.11	−.06
	$N =$	197	192	196	190	197	196	196	190	197
	$p =$	.05	N.S.	N.S.	N.S.	N.S.	N.S.	N.S.	N.S.	N.S.

*The higher the score, the higher is the measure of the variable, for example, the higher is the quantity, quality, or efficiency of production.
§Not significant

TABLE 4-5 *Effectiveness and Integration of the Elites, 10 Hospitals*

MEASURES OF INTEGRATION OF THE ELITES	EFFECTIVENESS MEASURES			
	OVERALL QUALITY OF PATIENT CARE	PREVALENCE OF ADAPTATION	PROMPTNESS OF ADAPTATION	FLEXIBILITY
Extent to which medical staff understands needs and problems of board of trustees	−.04*	.60	.64	−.25
Extent to which board of trustees understands needs and problems of medical staff	.19	.72	.67	−.39
Adequacy of communication from administrator to medical staff, as perceived by latter	.38	.57	.55	−.39
Adequacy of communication from administrator to board members, as perceived by latter	−.10	.57	.55	−.54
Extent of board of trustees' interest in hospital operations beyond financial aspects	.00	.67	.56	−.19
Extent of medical staff's interest in hospital operations beyond medical aspects	−.10	.27	.88	−.27

*Spearman rank-order correlations were used; $r_s \geqslant .56$, significant at .05 level; $r_s \geqslant .75$, significant at .01 level.

these sites. The data on the ten community hospitals, each of which contained three legally recognized elites—the board of trustees, the administrator, and the medical staff—do permit some study of this relationship (see Table 4-5). Only four aspects of effectiveness as we have defined it were measured in that study. The pattern of relationships was strikingly compatible with our findings in Chapter 3. The quality of patient care was not related to any measures of integration of the elites. Hospital care was more structured than was much of the work of NASA and Alpha Agency. The most important unstructured aspect was the initial medical diagnosis; actual care, however, was quickly reduced to routine through the physicians' orders. The remaining production problems were usually handled by the head nurses. As we showed in Chapter 3, the activities of top management were unrelated to the effectiveness of a structured production process. They were shown to be relevant to the adaptation process, however. Table 4-5 supports those findings: as integration of the elites increased, behavioral adaptation also increased. When the elites were integrated, vertical barriers within the organization were eliminated. The potential deviant could find no comforting barrier between himself and those who demanded his compliance to changes in routines. In addition, a united front among authorities greatly augmented the force and legitimacy of their orders to modify routines.

Although none of our findings about flexibility was statistically significant, there appears to have been a negative relationship between flexibility and integration of elites. This set of findings also conforms to those presented in Chapter 3; there we saw that hospital integration was not significantly related to flexibility but was related in the negative direction. Another piece is thus added to our accumulating evidence that a decentralized and segmented organization may be most capable of effective, unstructured responses to work overloads.

CONFIGURATIONS OF DECISION-MAKING AND CHARACTERISTICS OF ORGANIZATIONS AND ATTITUDES

How are decision-making structures related to other aspects of organizational behavior and the attitudes of the people involved in them? Table 4-6 shows some relationships with the

TABLE 4-6 *Relationships Between Perceived Decision-Making Structures and Other Organizational Variables*

	PERCEIVED LOCUS OF DECISION-MAKING	
ORGANIZATIONAL VARIABLES	CENTRAL-IZED	FAIRLY CENTRALIZED
Clarity of normative environment		
Clarity of work objectives	2.09*	3.10
	(2.47)†	(2.72)
Clarity of rules, policies, and guidelines	-	-
	(3.21)	(2.94)
Extent to which workers are given conflicting priorities	2.48	2.10
	(2.74)	(2.93)
Extent to which front office changes policies without advance notice	-	-
	(2.56)	(3.21)
Coordination		
How well related jobs are meshed to achieve objectives	2.80	3.59
	(2.53)	(3.26)
Conditions for negotiating orders		
Ease of exchanging ideas and information with others doing related work	2.57	3.59
	(2.58)	(3.63)
Extent to which people doing related work avoid creating problems for one another	2.78	3.70
	(2.89)	(3.88)
How well coordination problems with others doing related work are handled	2.80	3.63
	(2.84)	(3.43)
Levels of skills		
Proportion of personnel competent to do the division's work	-	-
	(3.79)	(4.06)
N, NASA-2	46	231
N, Alpha Agency	(20)	(259)

*Data from NASA-2.
†Data from Alpha Agency are shown in parentheses.
§Not significant.

major organizational characteristics examined in Chapter 3. The mean scores in Table 4-6 reveal the same underlying pattern that our earlier data showed: Generally no type of decision-making structure was related to other aspects of organization; whenever there was such a relation, it always involved the centralized configuration. (We have omitted the product-moment correlation coefficients, for not one of them was significant; they obdurately remained within a few hundredths of .00.) Respondents who perceived centralized decision-making structures in their divisions also reported the greatest difficulty in maintaining negotiated orders. This finding conforms with those of other studies of the effects of authoritarian lead-

PERCEIVED LOCUS OF DECISION-MAKING				
BAL-ANCED	FAIRLY DECENTRALIZED	DECENTRAL-IZED	F SCORE	P
2.92	3.00	2.91	6.40	.01
(2.61)	(1.93)	(3.18)	(3.06)	(.05)
-	-	-	-	-
(3.24)	(2.53)	(3.53)	(2.11)	(N.S.)§
2.63	2.20	2.39	1.94	N.S.
(3.24)	(3.43)	(2.72)	(2.04)	(N.S.)
-	-	-	-	-
(3.02)	(3.00)	(3.29)	(2.23)	(N.S.)
3.02	3.20	3.76	8.56	.01
(3.20)	(3.00)	(3.61)	(4.34)	(.01)
3.45	3.40	3.57	9.12	.01
(3.63)	(3.40)	(4.00)	(5.54)	(.01)
3.55	2.80	3.48	6.72	.01
(3.74)	(3.93)	(3.83)	(5.02)	(.01)
3.13	2.60	3.71	8.51	.01
(3.22)	(3.40)	(3.44)	(2.20)	(.01)
-	-	-	-	-
(4.17)	(3.87)	(4.28)	(1.06)	(N.S.)
41	5	23		
(47)	(15)	(19)		

ership styles on lateral communication.[12] In such organizations the use of formal channels and procedures is emphasized. The fundamental conception of how work should be organized is opposite to that of negotiated orders. Problem solving in informal subgroups is often discouraged because accountability for mistakes is more difficult to establish and because such groups are sometimes perceived by division directors as potential centers of opposing power.

[12]Hannah Arendt, *The Origins of Totalitarianism* (New York: Harcourt Brace Jovanovich, 1951); R. H. Guest, *Organizational Change: The Effect of Successful Leadership* (Homewood, Ill.: Dorsey, 1962), pp. 17-37; D. McGregor, *The Human Side of Enterprise* (New York: McGraw-Hill, 1960); and R. R. Blake and J. S. Mouton, *The Managerial Grid* (Houston: Gulf, 1964), pp. 57-80.

All measures of coordination in both the NASA-2 and Alpha Agency studies were related to the types of decision-making structure, in the same manner as shown in Table 4-6. Despite their penchant for formal coordination, authoritarian division directors had difficulty achieving it. Subordinates who reported that decision-making was centralized also reported that problems of coordination were not handled very well and that time was lost because of poor planning by supervisors. Centralized divisions are by definition heavily dependent upon their directors for achieving effective performance; if a director fails to perform the functions that would otherwise be achieved through negotiated orders, the performance of the division declines. Centralization of decision-making had its most negative effects on assessments of supervisory performance. Of the eighty-one questionnaire items related to the decision-making item in the NASA-1 data 93 percent of the supervisory items and 63 percent of the remaining items produced significant F-test scores. The comparable figures for the Alpha Agency study were 58 and 30 percent respectively. Centralized decision-making was always related to the most negative assessments of supervisory performance. The respondents either reported on division directors as their immediate supervisors or indicated that the performance of their supervisors was impaired by division directors. These situations will be analyzed in greater detail in Chapter 7.

Findings not shown in Table 4-6 can be summarized briefly. First, when respondents perceived that decision-making was centralized, they were more likely to be thinking of quitting, though they also reported that their divisions were able to keep enough competent people to do the work. They also reported less job satisfaction and more negative assessments of their own chances for promotion. They believed that top management was successful at forcing employees to meet its needs while failing to meet their needs and that the people in their units were trying to achieve high levels of performance.

Second, the fifteen people in Alpha Agency who reported that their divisions had fairly decentralized decision-making structures were also inclined to assess their supervisors negatively. The paucity of examples prevents analysis of the sources of these evaluations, but the finding does lead to some intriguing speculations that warrant further study.

Third, in all other respects there were no differences among configurations of decision-making in their effects on organizational behavior and attitudes.

LEGITIMACY OF DECISION-MAKING STRUCTURES AND EFFECTIVENESS

In the preceding discussion we assumed that the perceived legitimacy of a decision-making structure is an important factor in the individual's motivation to work effectively. We assumed, for example, that, when a worker who accepts the legitimacy of a fairly centralized structure is required to work in a decentralized one, his morale and performance will suffer. Confirmation of this assumption can be found in the literature of the social sciences. Max Weber in his discussion of types of authority[13] and Georg Simmel in his discussion of subordination to a principle[14] asserted its validity on purely theoretical grounds. Swanson proposed it as an explanatory variable in his study of decision-making groups that had undergone changes in their structures and had experienced subsequent reductions in effectiveness.[15] Because of the importance of this assumption and the inadequate evidence to support it, we incorporated a direct test of it in the Byberry-2 study. In addition to the usual question about how major decisions were actually made, the respondents in Byberry were asked:

Which of the following comes closest to describing how you feel the *important* decisions *should* be made in your department?

_____(1) The department head should make the important decisions. He rarely should ask for advice; he should just give orders.

_____(2) The department head should make the *final* decision, but should rely on other people in the department for advice and recommendations.

[13] Max Weber, *The Theory of Social Economic Organization*, 2nd ed., trans. A. M. Henderson and Talcott Parsons (New York: Free Press, 1947), pp. 324-423.

[14] Kurt Wolff, trans., *The Sociology of Georg Simmel* (New York: Free Press, 1950), pp. 250-267.

[15] Swanson, *op. cit.*

_____(3) Some important decisions should be made by the department head; but about as many should be made by others in the department.

_____(4) Several different people should make the important decisions. The department head shouldn't really have more influence than any of them.

_____(5) A number of people should be equally involved. They should usually get together and discuss the problem and agree on a solution.

Using these two measures of actual and preferred locus of decision-making, we were able to construct a disparity score for each respondent. When a respondent said that the decision-making structures was actually centralized and should be, he received a disparity score of 0.00. One who said it was centralized but should be decentralized received a score of 4.00 and so on. By this method all respondents who answered both questions were assigned disparity scores ranging from 0.00 to 4.00; the larger the score, the less the respondent believed that the perceived locus of decision-making in his department was legitimate. No attempt was made to indicate numerically the direction in which the respondent believed that legitimacy lay because the concept of legitimacy was defined only as the extent to which the existing decision-making structure was normative. Table 4-7 shows the distribution of responses to both questions among Byberry respondents who were directly

TABLE 4-7 *Distribution of Individual Responses to Questions About Actual and Preferred Loci of Decision-Making*, *Byberry-2*

| | ACTUAL LOCUS | | | | | |
PREFERRED LOCUS	CENTRALIZED	FAIRLY CENTRALIZED	BALANCED	FAIRLY DECENTRALIZED	DECENTRALIZED	N
Centralized	2*	0	0	0	1	3
Fairly centralized	6	63	16	5	6	96
Balanced	0	4	7	1	1	13
Fairly decentralized	4	1	0	0	0	5
Decentralized	8	11	2	3	13	37
N	20	79	25	9	21	154

*Two respondents said that the actual locus of decision-making was centralized and that it should be centralized.

involved in either treatment of the patients or administrative work.

The respondents did not show the great preference for a decentralized decision-making structure that Likert's studies of managers would have led us to expect.[16] Preference for the decentralized configuration was a weak second to that for the fairly centralized one, but this result is not very surprising. The generations of Americans currently predominant in the labor force have been socialized to accept a fairly centralized authority system as legitimate in most work situations. This expectation has been augmented in the hospital professions, which have a long history of hierarchical organization. Future generations may attribute legitimacy to other configurations; there is considerable evidence to suggest this possibility. But for now most people probably attribute legitimacy to the fairly centralized decision-making structure for most production and service organizations. It is equally clear that the centralized and fairly decentralized configurations were accorded legitimacy by very few respondents. From our follow-up interviews it was clear that the fairly decentralized model was equated with chaos because the vast majority of respondents expected hospitals to be run as well-defined authority systems and this expectation was their frame of reference for interpreting the items.

The disparity score was negatively related to the respondent's age ($r = -.27$) and length of service ($r = -.18$) in his present work unit; the younger he was and the shorter his service, the less likely he was to consider the perceived decision-making structure of his unit legitimate. Most young workers lack the experience, seniority, and reputation to share in decision-making as they may desire. The data show that they were more likely than were older workers to prefer a more decentralized decision-making structure ($r = .32$), but their perceptions of the actual loci of decision-making were no different from those of older workers ($r = -.07$). Table 4-8 shows how the disparity scores were related to various measures of effectiveness.

These data show a direct relationship between the legitimacy of the decision-making structure and its organizational

[16] Rensis Likert, *The Human Organization: Its Management and Value* (New York: McGraw-Hill, 1967), pp. 30-36.

TABLE 4-8 *Legitimacy and Organizational Effectiveness, Byberry-2*

MEASURES OF EFFECTIVENESS	PRODUCT MOMENT CORRELATIONS WITH DISPARITY SCORES (LEGITIMACY)
Index of overall effectiveness	−.27*
Index of productivity	−.31
Index of adaptability	−.24
Measure of flexibility	.03
Productivity	
Quantity	−.41
Quality	−.23
Efficiency	−.20
Adaptability	
Anticipating problems	−.23
Keeping up to date	−.07
Promptness	−.09
Prevalence	−.24
Making patients comfortable	−.27
Giving patients adequate personal attention	−.20

*The average number of cases for each correlation was 151; $r = .16$, significant at .05 level; $r \leqslant .21$ at .01 level.

effectiveness. As legitimacy declined, the workers' motivation to produce and contribute to the activities of the organization probably declined with it. This explanation is suggested by a number of findings. For example, the greater the disparity score, the less likely respondents were to report that their units worked hard or that others were likely to help them with their duties and responsibilities. This decline in motivation probably accounts for the strong relationship between legitimacy and quantity of production. Flexibility was probably unrelated to legitimacy because the worker's concern for the safety of his patients probably overrode the negative motivational effects of low legitimacy. As we have already seen, unstructured flexibility is a function of professionalism, length of service, commitment to professional standards of behavior, and previous experience with similar emergencies.

CONCLUSIONS

Some very important insights into human organizations have been obscured by the common penchant among social scientists for including social values in their definitions of social power, as if power were used only for social objectives. Equally troublesome has been the common tendency to define power as some situation in which values are *never* operative. If we maintain conceptual distinctness between power and social values or goals, we can conceptualize social power as an instrument used in particular situations for socially valued objectives, egoistic purposes, or both. Under what conditions is it used for each type of objective? Are there highly centralized configurations in which the elite uses power in socially valued ways to pursue generally acceptable objectives? It is, in fact, conceivable that any configuration of power can be associated or unassociated with the legitimate pursuit of social goals.

Why, then, have so many social scientists, particularly those in the human relations tradition, assumed that legitimacy and morality are associated only with a decentralized configuration of power or decision-making? Much of the answer derives from the fact that in the United States the use of social power has been relatively unconstrained by social values. Externally imposed laws have here and there replaced the older traditional norms that governed organizations before industrialization and the convenient doctrine of laissez-faire. The social use of industrial-commercial organizations has been foreign to our times. But other organizations—political, governmental, and even religious—are frequently perceived as operating without the constraints of social values.

Organizations are, however, composed of people; if organizations are less constrained today by social values, then so are the people in them, particularly the key decision-makers. People frequently use authority, regardless of the configuration of authority, to pursue egoistic objectives. Under such anomic conditions the centralization of power becomes especially undesirable. An all-powerful elite pursuing its egoistic objectives at the frequent expense of the less powerful is attractive to few people. The demand that power be shared is at least a defensive move. Furthermore, it is conceivable that anomic power attracts the hostile or authoritarian personality, whereas power constrained by social values does not. These reasons are probably part of the explanation of why organizational effectiveness and individual morale are so little related to centralized configurations of decision-making; not the configuration itself but the fact that it is unconstrained by social values controls the relationship. The leader is free to use the organization for the fulfillment of its social mission and the development of personnel, for personal aggrandizement, or as a structured system of defense against the objects of his anxieties. He is free to abuse his personnel or to treat them well. The choice is his. The real issue then is not how to decentralize decision-making but, rather, how to reintroduce constraints of social values on the configurations of power.

Some of the grosser characteristics of cultural systems necessary to constrain the decision-making system and to augment the effectiveness of work groups were discussed in Chapter 3. The normative environment should be characterized by clarity. The objectives toward which to work and the norms governing performance should be clear. The individual probably prefers that these objectives and norms be reasonable and fair. We have no evidence that all these attributes are necessary parts of the normative environment other than the indirect evidence of our findings about rational-trust leadership. Obviously this area is a critical one for further research. Under what conditions is the exercise of power constrained or unconstrained by social values? What are the attributes of the social values most significantly related to organizational and to individual effectiveness?

5
Organizational Needs,
Individual Needs, and
Organizational Effectiveness

As we saw in Chapter 1 both the open and closed approaches to human organizations involve assumptions about the people that live and work in them. Because of their emphasis on structure, closed-system theorists make as few assumptions about individuals as they can. In their industrial applications these theories have often included vague or simplistic notions about individuals and their motivations to work. Some have assumed that people are inherently motivated to work; others have thought that motivations to work are triggered by appropriate systems of rewards and punishments or by environments structured so as not to *prevent* people from doing the work that they are assigned. Still others, more cognizant of the importance of human personality in work relations, have favored selecting a man with the intelligence, manual skills, and so on to fit each job; when such selection has been successful, the structural approach to human organizations has been believed to have overcome one of its major disadvantages.

At the other extreme is the view that organizations will be most effective when first priority is given to the needs of individuals, that helping individuals to realize their potentials increases their motivation to work. But, within this framework, there is notable disagreement about which individual needs are related to self-actualization and high levels of performance: pay, job security, advancement, interesting work, opportunities to use personal skills, or others.

The views of most students of organizations are located along the continuum between these extremes. Most recognize that any extreme theory of organizational effectiveness is inevitably inadequate because both organizations and individuals

103

are palpably parts of the object of study. But, in order to maximize effectiveness, should organizational or individual needs be emphasized? Should the two be equally emphasized, as R. R. Blake and J. S. Mouton assume in *The Managerial Grid*?[1] Finding some answers to these questions is our major task in this chapter.

THE NASA-1 FINDINGS

The following pair of questions were asked of all respondents in the first study at the National Aeronautics and Space Administration:

How successful has NASA been in getting you to meet its needs—for example, getting you to produce what they want, when they want it, in the manner they want?

1%	(1) They have not been successful at all at getting me to meet NASA's needs
2%	(2) Not too successful
8%	(3) Somewhat successful
34%	(4) Fairly successful
51%	(5) They have been very successful at getting me to meet NASA's needs
4%	(8) Not ascertained

How good a job has NASA done at meeting your needs—for example, interesting work, adequate pay, a chance to use or develop your talents, or whatever it is that you want from your job?

9%	(1) NASA has not done a good job at all at meeting my needs
17%	(2) Not too good a job
35%	(3) A fair job
28%	(4) A very good job
10%	(5) NASA has done an excellent job at meeting my needs
1%	(8) Not ascertained

The percentage distributions shown are those for all respondents in the NASA-1 study. (The distribution of responses to these questions in the NASA-2 study was almost identical.)

[1] R. R. Blake and J. S. Mouton, *The Managerial Grid* (Houston: Gulf, 1964).

Obviously the respondents thought that NASA had been far more successful at persuading them to meet its needs than it was at meeting their needs. This finding fits our own impressions from two and a half years of observations and interviews in this organization. Performance standards and accountability systems were highly developed and rigorously enforced. The Director of the Office of Administration acknowledged on several occasions that he thought that he had pushed the classic administrative science approach about as far as it could be pushed. Our presence in his office partly reflected his interest in developing other approaches to organizational management.

The skewed distribution of responses to the item on organizational needs frustrated our desire to create a three-by-three table using these two questions. (That format requires a distribution of responses on the organizational-needs item more like that obtained on the individual-needs item.) We therefore designed a variation (see Table 5-1). The numbers in each cell represent the respondents who selected the pair of responses indicated; 154 respondents said that NASA was "fairly" or "very" successful at persuading them to meet its needs *and* that NASA had done an "excellent" or "good" job at meeting their needs.

TABLE 5-1 *Distribution of Responses to the Organizational- and Individual-Needs Items, NASA-1*

| | | ORGANIZATIONAL NEEDS MET | |
		HIGH (OPTIONS 4,5)	LOW (OPTIONS 1-3)
	High (Options 4,5)	154	10
Individual Needs Met	Medium (Option 3)	129	21
	Low (Options 1,2)	89	18

Table 5-2 shows how the respondents in each category evaluated the effectiveness of their own divisions. Several findings should be noted. First, the F test for all six mean scores was highly significant; the differences between the highest and lowest mean scores were thus also statistically significant. Second, the more the respondent thought that his needs were being met, the more effective he reported his work group to be.

TABLE 5-2 *Organizational and Individual Needs and Overall Effectiveness, NASA-1*

		ORGANIZATIONAL NEEDS MET	
		HIGH	LOW
Individual Needs Met	High	3.97*	3.55
	Medium	3.66	3.23
	Low	3.40	2.99

*Mean score on overall effectiveness index for respondents in this category, $F = 17.20; p < .01$.

Third, the more he thought that NASA was successful at persuading him to meet its needs, the more effective he reported his work group to be. Fourth, two-way analysis of variance shows that the findings on organizational needs account for more variation in the effectiveness measure than do those on individual needs (F = 20.15 and 10.66 respectively). This result suggests that at NASA high divisional effectiveness was achieved by meeting both individual and organizational needs, with somewhat greater emphasis on the latter.

This last statement is supported by the data shown in Table 5-3. The data from Alpha Agency are also included here. Both items on fulfillment of needs were statistically related to effectiveness but did not account for much variance in the latter. Nor did they account for much of each other's variance. A multiple correlation coefficient combining both items explained more variance in effectiveness but not much more than was explained by organizational needs alone. Together the items on fulfillment of needs accounted for only 10 percent of the variance in effectiveness.[2]

The pattern of responses shown in Table 5-2 for the

[2] The possibility that these results are the consequence of the operation of other variables was checked. The prime suspect was respondents' G.S. levels; it was conceivable that higher-level personnel might evaluate effectiveness, as well as fulfillment of their own needs, more highly. But G. S. level was not related to either of these measures. Some items in the effectiveness measure were significantly related to respondents' G. S. level, but the relations were both direct and inverse, cancelling each other in the summary measure. There was a trend in the expected direction, in the relationship between fulfillment of individual needs and G. S. level, but it was not significant ($X^2 = 3.91$, $d.f. = 2$, $p = .15$). In Alpha Agency this relationship was highly significant ($X^2 = 20.57$, $d.f. = 2$, $p < .001$). None of the other background variables examined produced statistically significant relationships or even tendencies.

TABLE 5-3 *Product-Moment Correlations Among Items on Fulfilling Organizational-Individual Needs and on Effectiveness*

	NASA-1	ALPHA AGENCY
r_{12}	.26*	.30
r_{13}	.22	.25
r_{23}	.15	.10
$r_{1.23}$	.32	.36
$r_{12.3}$	.23	.28
$r_{13.2}$	.19	.23

*All correlations were significant at .05 level or higher; $N > 400$; 1 = overall effectiveness index; 2 = organizational needs met; 3 = individual needs met.

overall effectiveness index was repeated exactly for each of its component measures; the productivity, adaptability, and flexibility indexes. There was only one minor variation. The respondents who reported that neither their needs nor those of NASA were being met scored the behavioral adaptation items as highly as did others who felt more positively. They also reported that they had the most authoritarian supervisors. Apparently these supervisors were able to extract behavioral conformity but not symbolic adaptation from their subordinates.

ALPHA AGENCY FINDINGS

The same two questions were asked in Alpha Agency and the distribution of responses was as follows:

How successful has the top management of (Alpha Agency) been in getting you to produce what they want, when they want it, in the manner they want?

1%	(1) They have not been successful at all at getting me to meet the (agency needs)
5%	(2) Not too successful
12%	(3) Somewhat successful
42%	(4) Fairly successful
32%	(5) They have been very successful
8%	(8) Not ascertained

How good a job has (Alpha Agency) done at meeting your needs—for example, promotions, interesting work, adequate pay, a chance to use or develop your talents, or whatever it is you want from your job?

6%	(1) (Alpha Agency) has not done a good job at all at meeting my needs
14%	(2) Not too good a job
30%	(3) A fair job
30%	(4) A very good job
17%	(5) (Alpha Agency) has done an excellent job at meeting my needs
3%	(8) Not ascertained

These distributions are fairly comparable to those from NASA. Alpha Agency appears to have been more successful, as was NASA, at having its needs met than at meeting the needs of its personnel, but on neither dimension were its scores as extreme as were those of NASA.

A two-by-three table similar to Table 5-1 was constructed for the Alpha Agency data, and the mean scores of responses to the effectiveness measures were examined in each of the six categories of the table. Essentially the same pattern of results as for the NASA-1 data was obtained. The highest effectiveness scores were given uniformly when both organizational and individual needs were met most successfully. The lowest scores were given when the opposite conditions were reported. Again respondents who reported that their needs were seldom, if ever, met also reported that their divisions were relatively centralized. But the same respondents also reported the lowest behavioral, as well as symbolic, adaptation: the only finding that varied from the NASA-1 findings.

INDIVIDUAL NEEDS AND EFFECTIVENESS

That every individual brings to his job a repertoire of needs that is in some respects unique is obvious and well documented.[3] That large organizations do not satisfy all the needs of all their members seems equally obvious. The problem is which individual needs should management meet in order to facilitate the development of an effective organization? To obtain some answers to this question, we submitted this pair of questions to the respondents in NASA-1:

Listed below are different kinds of opportunities which

[3] For an excellent summary of the research on the subject of individual needs, Phillip B. Applewhite, *Organizational Behavior* (Englewood Cliffs, N.J.: Prentice-Hall, 1965), pp. 6-35.

a job might afford. If you were to seek another job, how much importance would you personally attach to each of these (disregarding whether or not your present job provides them)?

Importance I would attach

Check one in each line	Slight or None (1)	Moderate (2)	Considerable (3)	Great (4)	Utmost (5)
A. to make full use of my knowledge and skills	___	___	___	___	___
B. to earn a good salary	___	___	___	___	___
C. to advance in authority and status	___	___	___	___	___
D. to be a member of a hard-working team	___	___	___	___	___
E. to work for competent, fair supervisors	___	___	___	___	___
F. to associate with important people in the organization	___	___	___	___	___
G. to work on difficult and challenging problems	___	___	___	___	___
H. to have freedom to carry out my own ideas	___	___	___	___	___
I. to have clear objectives toward which to aim my work	___	___	___	___	___
J. to be evaluated fairly in proportion to what I contribute	___	___	___	___	___
K. to have job security	___	___	___	___	___
L. to have a lot of responsibility	___	___	___	___	___

This question was designed to discover the importance that each respondent attached to the needs listed in the stub;

a second, similar question was designed to discover to what extent respondents' jobs fulfilled the same list of needs.[4] It was then possible to compare what an individual wanted from his job with what he thought that he received. Table 5-4 shows the results of this analysis.

Several observations can be made from this table. First, it is striking that the needs deemed most important were for full use of knowledge and skills, competent and fair supervision, fair evaluation, clear objectives toward which to work, challenging problems, and membership in a hard-working team. The respondents generally showed no unwillingness to work hard. They preferred a rational, fair, "knowable" normative environment of the type discussed in the conclusions to Chapter 3. Second, these six greatest needs were among the eight for which NASA made the least provision, according to respondents. Third, the same six needs were among the seven that were most highly correlated with division effectiveness. *The individual needs for which the least provision was made by NASA were thus those that made the greatest contribution to divisional effectiveness.* One possible explanation for this finding is that the respondents rated the effectiveness of their division low *because* their needs were not fulfilled, but the Alpha Agency data do not support this conclusion. The six need items most highly related to effectiveness in the NASA-1 study were used again in Alpha Agency. The extent to which these needs were fulfilled was still highly related to effectiveness, [5] but the disparities between importance and fulfillment were

[4] Floyd C. Mann, Center Director of the Institute for Social Research, developed these questions from his own research and that reported in F. Herzberg, B. Mauser and B. Snyderman, *The Motivation to Work* (New York: J. Wiley, 1959); and M. Scott Myers, "Who Are Your Motivated Workers?" *Harvard Business Review*, 42 (January-February 1964), 73-88.

[5] The scores for Alpha Agency and for Byberry-2 are shown in this table.

	ALPHA	BYBERRY-2
Use of knowledge and skills	$r = .26$	.25
Membership in a hard-working team	.48	.39
Competent and fair supervision	.42	*
Freedom to carry out own ideas	.23	.26
Clear objectives toward which to work	.35	.33
Fair evaluation	.34	*

*This item was not included in this study.

TABLE 5-4 Comparison of Importance and Provision of Needs with Divisional Effectiveness, NASA-1

| OCCUPATIONAL NEEDS | (1) IMPORTANCE OF OCCUPATIONAL NEEDS | MEAN SCORES FOR ALL RESPONDENTS | | CORRELATION OF (2) WITH OVERALL EFFECTIVENESS |
		(2) ACTUAL FULFILLMENT OF NEEDS	(2) MINUS (1)	
Full use of knowledge and skills	4.21*	2.95†	−1.26	.36§
Clear objectives toward which to work	3.82	2.66	−1.16	.45
Advancement in authority and status	3.15	2.01	−1.14	.21
Fair evaluation	4.00	2.88	−1.12	.32
Freedom to carry out own ideas	3.65	2.63	−1.02	.28
Challenging problems	3.78	2.78	−1.00	.25
Competent and fair supervision	4.18	3.20	−0.98	.34
Membership in a hard-working team	3.74	2.90	−0.84	.40
A good salary	3.69	3.06	−0.63	.08
Lots of responsibility	3.19	2.65	−0.54	.15
Job security	3.34	3.30	−0.04	.04
Association with important people in the organization	2.32	2.30	−0.02	−.09

*The higher the mean score, the more important is the need.
†The higher the mean score, the more the need is fulfilled.
§Product-moment correlations were used; $N > 400$; $r \geqslant .10$ is significant at .05 level; $r \geqslant .13$ is significant at .01 level.

less than half as large. The exception was the clear-objectives item, on which there was a fairly large disparity, as at NASA. If the explanation offered were correct, there would be little or no relationship between fulfillment of needs and effectiveness of Alpha Agency.

A more likely explanation arises when we take these items and the responses at face value. The data conform rather closely to Frederick Herzberg's propositions relating human needs to work situations. Herzberg has divided human needs into two types: hygiene and motivator needs.[6] Safety, security, and comfort are hygiene needs that can be satisfied in our society by pay increases, promotions, and job seniority. But these "satisfiers" have only temporary effects; after each promotion or salary increase the individual feels less dissatisfied for a while, but then he wants another. Not only is this satisfaction temporary, it also produces no increased productivity. Satisfying hygiene needs does not therefore increase the effectiveness of the work group.

But typically the individual also has another set of needs for personal or psychological and social growth. He wants to derive a sense of worth, or self-esteem, from his various activities and roles. He wants to perform his roles as spouse and parent so that they are rewarding to others and to himself. If a role does not provide him with opportunities for personal growth, he will usually try to avoid it, devalue its importance, or develop negative emotional reactions. Self-esteem can be derived from work as from any other role or activity; most individuals want to invest themselves in their work and to be able to define themselves partly by the products of their efforts. They want opportunities to use the full range of their knowledge and skills because these opportunities can increase their sense of self-worth. They need freedom to carry out their own ideas, to work on challenging problems, and to be parts of hard-working teams for the same reasons.

There was a relationship between fulfillment of these needs and effectiveness of the work group. When work permits people to use their knowledge and skills and to cope with challenging problems as parts of hard-working teams, their energies and creativity are unleashed; they are not encumbered

[6] Frederick Herzberg, *Work and the Nature of Man* (Cleveland: World, 1966), especially pp. 71-91.

in ways that cause them to do less than they are capable of doing. The work group is thus very likely to be more effective than when these needs are not met.

Other needs related to effectiveness reflect desire for rational, fair, and "knowable" environments. The individual wants to be evaluated according to his achievements, not according to vague, capricious, or constantly changing standards that threaten his sense of security. Furthermore, when the environment is rational, fair, and "knowable," then, as we saw in Chapter 3 the worker has a repertoire of objectives with which to guide his own activities and is likely to make fewer false starts in his work.

Many behavioral scientists have for some time recognized the importance of these motivating needs in individual development. This recognition is being expressed in new management systems or processes whose characteristics include involving the worker in setting objectives for himself and his work unit, giving him an opportunity to develop his own work plans to achieve the objectives that he and his supervisor have agreed upon, appraisal according to the results that he has achieved, and developing supervisors and managers who can coach and counsel their personnel adequately and provide them with job enrichment and growth opportunities. Management systems of this type are very likely to meet individuals' needs for autonomy, self-esteem from work, and a rational environment. Our data also show that they are likely to enhance the effectiveness of the organization.

It is important, however, to resist the implication that salary and promotional opportunities are not important. They are. It is true that they are often sought when the work situation does not permit much fulfillment of other individual needs. Workers often seek higher pay as a reward for putting up with the unpleasantness of their work or to support interests in other areas of their lives. They may seek promotions in the hope that higher up it will be better than where they are. But even when the environment is nearly ideal most individuals still attach great importance to their pay and promotional opportunities. Work is not the only area of an individual's life from which he derives self-esteem: Potentially he can derive it from all areas of his life. His salary is one major way that he can afford those activities and acquisitions that give meaning to the other areas of his life, and promotions may bring greater responsibility and chances to work on larger problems. On the other hand, it is really unfortunate when an individual who likes his current work seeks a promotion as a way to escape or control a work environment that he finds intolerable.

In most places of work every one of the individual needs that is highly related to organizational effectiveness can be implemented by managers without additional resources from their superiors. Many managers, including many of the division directors whom we studied, lament that their resources are inadequate to meet the needs of their subordinates, but they are usually thinking of pay and promotional opportunities. This error is understandable, for people frequently seek these rewards whether their work and their work situation are good or bad. Our research and other, similar efforts [7] have shown, however, that there are individual needs to which people attach even greater importance than they attach to salary and promotional opportunities, needs related to organizational effectiveness. Except in highly closed situations like assembly lines, supervisors usually have all the authority and resources necessary to fulfill many of these needs. They can involve their personnel in setting objectives for themselves and their work group, develop their own plans to achieve their objectives, appraise them according to the results they achieve, and so forth. The ultimate irony, then, is that they may have misunderstood what their personnel want from jobs and have been the least successful at providing for the needs that contribute most to work-group effectiveness.

CONCLUSIONS

The data in this chapter suggest that managers and supervisors can increase the effectiveness of their organizations by fulfilling certain individual, as well as organizational, needs. At the sites NASA, Alpha Agency, and Byberry the effectiveness of units was greater when ample provision was made for personally challenging work; rational, fair, and "knowable" normative environments; and competent and fair supervisors. These characteristics were also shown to have been less prevalent in these organizations than were the other characteristics studied in this chapter.

[7] Applewhite, *op. cit.*, pp. 6-35.

This consistent low fulfillment of needs related to effectiveness raises some interesting questions. If these needs are so important, why have they not been met? Are managers simply unaware of their importance? Does type of technology affect the ability to fulfill needs for self-actualization? Is work so structured that freedom to carry out individual ideas or to make full use of individual knowledge and skills is impossible? Equally intriguing, why are normative environments so limited in rationality, fairness, and "knowability"? The frailties of the communication process, lack of time to interact sufficiently, and occasional perceived intimidations based on status differences are all known to minimize development of the desirable normative environment. But are there not some short-run advantages to the manager from normative confusion or vagueness? He can implement different values with different subordinates, keep them confused and relatively powerless, and thus minimize constraints on his own behavior. Social scientists should at least examine more carefully the reasons why some managers will not strive for effective normative environments even when they know that their own are inadequate.

6
Leadership
and
Organizational Effectiveness

This chapter was prepared especially for this volume by D. Anthony Butterfield, who worked on our NASA projects. The measures necessary for his doctoral dissertation were included in the NASA-1 study, and in this chapter he summarizes some of his findings. A more complete presentation can be found in D. A. Butterfield, "An Integrative Approach to the Study of Leadership Effectiveness in Organizations" (Doctoral diss., The University of Michigan, 1968).

Among the many variables used to predict and understand organizational effectiveness, leadership is central. Indeed, the supervisor's behavior is often considered the key element in how effectively a group will perform. The search for the proper type of leadership *behavior* replaced the search for the ideal leader per se. The basic questions became: What are the important kinds of leadership behavior? And how are they related to group effectiveness?

There has been no lack of attempts to answer these questions. The data in this chapter were gathered to test four theories that have been put forth. Although developed by different investigators, these theories have a great deal in common, partly because the investigators were colleagues at the University of Michigan Institute for Social Research. Each theory is, however, based on a slightly different view of leadership and its relationship to organizational effectiveness.

Floyd Mann has proposed a *skill mix* of human relations, technical matters, administration, and more recently institutional leadership. The appropriate mixture of skills varies with organizational level.[1] Rensis Likert's *system IV* organization is based

[1]F. C. Mann, "Toward an Understanding of the Leadership Role in Formal Organization," in *Leadership and Productivity*, ed. R. Dubin, F. Mann, and D. Miller (San Francisco: Chandler, 1965), pp. 68-103.

on such supervisory principles as supportive relationships, high performance goals, group methods, and participation.[2] D. G. Bowers and S. E. Seashore have suggested that the latter two approaches, along with earlier work at Michigan and Ohio State University, involve primarily *four factors* of leadership: support, emphasis on goals, facilitation of interaction, and facilitation of work.[3] Each of these three approaches has been subjected to some form of empirical testing, though not comparatively. A fourth approach has been suggested by D. Katz and R. L. Kahn. They have posited *three patterns* of leadership, corresponding approximately to organizational levels, each with a cognitive and an affective element.[4] This model has yet to undergo direct empirical testing.

A NOTE ON DESIGN

Before describing these leadership theories—and the associated variables—in more detail, we note that two of them suggest that organizational level is important in determining which types of leadership behavior are related to effectiveness. Do effective higher-level supervisors exhibit the same supervisory behavior that effective lower-level supervisors do? Obviously, it was necessary to gather data from two levels of the National Aeronautics and Space Administration—division and branch— for our leadership analyses.[5] Data on supervisory behavior were collected in the same manner as were the data on negotiating orders coordination, and so on already described in earlier chapters—except that respondents reporting directly to division directors described their division directors on the supervisory items, whereas those reporting to branch chiefs described their branch chiefs. In this way data about two levels of leadership were obtained.

Obtaining data on effectiveness at the branch level was more difficult. The effectiveness index that had proved so reliable as a measure of division performance was not appli-

---

[2] R. Likert, *The Human Organization: Its Management and Value* (New York: McGraw-Hill, 1967).

[3] D. G. Bowers and S. E. Seashore, "Predicting Organizational Effectiveness with a Four-Factor Theory of Leadership," *Administrative Science Quarterly*, 11 (1966): 238-263.

[4] D. Katz and R. L. Kahn, "Leadership," in *The Social Psychology of Organizations*, ed. Katz and Kahn (New York: Wiley, 1966), pp. 300-335.

[5] A branch is a subunit of a division; branch chiefs report to division directors.

cable at the branch level because the questionnaire was geared to division production, division efficiency, and so on, rather than to branch performance. With a few exceptions branch scores on the effectiveness index were usually not significantly different from one another within the same division. It was therefore necessary to find an independent measure of branch effectiveness.

We obtained rankings from judges familiar with the work of the different branches, much as we had obtained rankings of division effectiveness to validate the questionnaire index. A total of ten division directors and twenty branch chiefs independently ranked overall branch effectiveness. The combined rank order produced by the division directors correlated ($r = .63$)[6] with the combined rank order produced by the branch chiefs. N was twenty-nine branches,[7] and $r = .63$ was thus significant well beyond the .01 probability level. The branch effectiveness scores used in our leadership analyses were average rankings of division directors and branch chiefs combined.

To facilitate comparison of results from the two organizational levels, we shall use both the index of overall effectiveness described in Chapter 2 and the division rankings in correlations with supervisory behavior of division directors. Applying both criteria at the division level allows a better assessment of the importance of differences in criteria.

LEADERSHIP THEORIES AND VARIABLES

Mann's "Skill Mix"

Mann has proposed a conceptual framework centered on the idea of different skill requirements for leadership at different organizational levels at different times. He has argued that no single skill is of overriding importance; rather, it is the "skill mix" that counts.

Mann views the supervisor's role as that of coordinator of two sets of interrelations. From a sociological and structural point of view, the supervisor coordinates the work of the unit

6 Ranks were converted to scores suitable for computing Pearson product-moment correlations; see Henry S. Garret, *Statistics in Psychology and Education*, 3rd ed. (New York: Longmans, 1947), pp. 172f. The correlation is therefore expressed as r rather than as Greek rho.

7 Although there were twenty-nine branches, there were only twenty-eight supervisors; N for the branch level will therefore be 28 in subsequent analyses.

that he supervises with that of the rest of the organization. From a social-psychological and motivational point of view, he coordinates the goals of individual members with those of the organization. As we shall see, these two sets of coordinating duties are not unlike the cognitive and affective requirements of Katz and Kahn.

To fulfill these two types of coordinating functions, the supervisor draws upon three kinds of supervisory skills: human-relations, technical, and administrative skills. More recently Mann has added a fourth, "institutional skill", which is relevant primarily at upper organizational levels. [8]

Human-relations skills involve working effectively with people, understanding and using principles of interpersonal relations and human motivation. They are necessary if one is to recognize and integrate the goals of individuals with those of the organization. "Basically,...(human relations skill) involves managing the emotional and motivational dimensions of interpersonal relations in an organization." [9] *Technical skills* are required for the particular tasks of the work group. The ability to use pertinent knowledge, methods, techniques, and equipment in performing and directing work activities is basic. Technical skills include both cognitive understanding and proficiency in performance. *Administrative skills* are necessary in coordinating the work of the group with the total organizational system. Planning and scheduling work, making job assignments, monitoring, and coordinating work with that of other work units require administrative skills. *Institutional skills* are used in adjusting the organization to its environment both internal and external. They include the ability to create and establish policy, understanding forces at work in the larger society particularly as they relate to the organization and the ability to represent the organization before other groups.

At the lower organizational levels, technical skills are considered most important; the ideal skill mix at those levels includes technical, human-relations, and administrative skills in that order. As we move up the hierarchy, administrative skills increase in importance, and institutional skills enter the picture. At the top the ideal skill mix includes strong components of administrative and institutional skills relative to the

[8] Personal communication.
[9] Mann, *op. cit.*, p. 75.

technical and human-relations types; the last are theoretically less important because motivation presents less of a problem at the top level. A minimum degree of each skill is considered necessary at all levels, but the mix is what counts most.

The items used to measure the skill-mix variables were identical with those previously used by Mann. Subordinates described their supervisors' behavior by checking one of five fixed responses, typically ranging from "little or no extent" (assigned a value of 1) to "very great extent" (assigned a value of 5). Each supervisor's score on each variable was simply the mean of the scores given him by his subordinates. In items designed to test the skill-mix theory, subordinates were asked to make fairly summary judgments on one item. In those testing the other theories, an index of several items was used to measure a given variable, and the final index score was the average of the scores on the several items.

Measures of Skill Mix
1. *Human relations skills* (single item). "How well does your supervisor handle the human relations side of his job—for example, getting people to work well together, getting individuals to do the best they can, giving recognition for good work done, letting people know where they stand, etc.?"
2. *Technical skills* (single item). "How well does your supervisor handle the technical side of his job—for example, general expertness, knowledge of job, technical skills needed, etc.?"
3. *Administrative skills* (single item). "How well does your supervisor handle the administrative side of his job—for example, planning and scheduling the work, indicating clearly when work is to be finished, assigning the right job to the right man, inspecting and following up on the work that is done, etc.?"
4. *Institutional skills* (single item). "How well does your supervisor handle the institutional leadership side of his job—for example, creating and formulating policy; handling matters of the agency's relationships to outside organizations, agencies, and groups; understanding the importance and relationships of the agency's mission on the political, social, and economic environment?"

Bowers and Seashore's Four-Factor Theory

After reviewing work on leadership done at Ohio State and Michigan, Bowers and Seashore concluded that the multitude of supervisory behaviors studied at those institutions could be organized on four basic dimensions of leadership: support, emphasis on goals, facilitation of interaction, and facilitation of work. *Support* is behavior that enhances someone else's feeling of personal worth and importance. *Emphasis on goals* stimulates enthusiasm for achieving the group's goal of excellent performance. *Facilitation of interaction* involves encouraging members of the group to develop close, mutually satisfying relationships. *Facilitation of work* is behavior that promotes attainment of goals by means of such activities as scheduling, coordinating, and planning and by means of such resources as tools, materials, and technical knowledge.

Bowers and Seashore have suggested that these dimensions represent activities that can be performed by anyone, not necessarily only the supervisor. Group members can supply leadership for one another in much the same way that the supervisor supplies it. Bowers and Seashore have pointed out that such "peer leadership" in no way renders formal supervision unnecessary. Their hypothesis of peer leadership, though not new in itself, represents an extension into field study of phenomena of influence that have long been studied by small-group researchers in the laboratory. In fact, this point is more than a hypothesis for Bowers and Seashore. They obtained measures of peer leadership, as well as of "managerial" leadership, on the four dimensions. In our study, however, we measured the leadership behavior only of supervisors, not of peers also.

Measures of the Four Factors

1. *Support* (three-item index). "Do you feel that your supervisor will go to bat or stand up for you? How free do you feel to discuss important things about your job with your supervisor? Would you describe your supervisor as approachable (easy to talk with) or distant (not easy to talk with)?"

2. *Emphasis on goals* (two-item index). "To what extent does your supervisor encourage extra effort? To what extent does your supervisor maintain high standards of performance?"

3. *Facilitation of interaction* (two-item index). "How much does your supervisor encourage the members of your work group to work together as a team? Does your supervisor deal with his subordinates on a man-to-man basis, or does he deal with them primarily as a group?"
4. *Facilitation of work* (four-item index). [10] "To what extent does your supervisor show you how to improve your performance? How frequently is work time lost because your supervisor fails to do the proper planning and scheduling?"

The indexes of support and work facilitation included items very similar to ones used in earlier four-factor research, and the goal-emphasis items were identical with those used earlier. The first interaction-facilitation item also replicated one used in four-factor studies, but the second was new in such research.

Katz and Kahn's Three-Pattern Approach

In 1966 Katz and Kahn set forth their view of organizations as open systems, imperfect ones at that, in which leadership is needed. They defined leadership as "any act of influence on a matter of organizational relevance"[11] and emphasized the importance of bases of influence not decreed by the organization. Expert power and referent power, which depend upon personal qualities of the leader rather than upon qualities inherent in the position itself, were considered a valuable adjunct to, if not a replacement for, power to reward and punish and legitimate authority.

According to this theory, every source of power may be used to exercise leadership of three different types: *origination* (creation, change, and elimination of structure), *interpolation* (supplementing and piecing out structure), and *administration* (using structure as it already exists). The three types correspond approximately to the top, middle, and bottom levels of organization.

For each of these levels of leadership Katz and Kahn have suggested a cognitive and an affective requirement:

[10] This index also included the "technical skills" and "administrative skills," items from the measures of skill mix. The planning item quoted here was scored in reverse.

[11] Katz and Kahn, *op. cit.*, p. 334.

1. Origination — A. *Systemic perspective* is the cognitive requirement for the highest pattern of leadership. It involves awareness of the organization's relationship with its environment—its impact on society and other institutions—changes in markets, long-range objectives, and so on. It also includes awareness of the interrelations among organizational subsystems and the ability to change or create new structure. Establishing and changing overall organizational policies are part of systemic perspective, which is quite similar to institutional skill as defined for the skill-mix approach.

1. Origination — B. *Charisma* is the affective requirement of top level leadership. It is an aura surrounding a leader that separates him (though not entirely) from the general membership. It arises from his ability to satisfy the dependency needs of his followers through dramatic leadership acts. Immediate subordinates are generally much less influenced by charisma than are followers more removed from the leader. No quantitative measure of charisma was taken in our study.

2. Interpolation — A. *Subsystem perspective* is the cognitive requirement at the middle level, the level of interpolation. It helps in implementing policy directives from above and in coordinating interdependent subsystems and thus requires both an upward and a downward orientation. To make effective use of subsystem perspective, the manager must be a good problem solver, a good coordinator, and influential with both his superiors and his subordinates.

2. Interpolation — B. *Ability to integrate primary and secondary relationships* is the affective requirement for middle-level leadership. It involves the practice of good human relations *in harmony with* organizational objectives, as the supervisor strives to make performance of organizational roles personally meaningful by aligning individual needs and work goals and activities more closely. He recognizes the importance of interpersonal relations and may build groups that provide social-psychological rewards as they perform organizational tasks.

3. Administration—A. *Technical knowledge of the job and knowledge of organizational rules* are the cognitive re-

quirements for bottom-level leadership. Technical skills are necessary for adequate direction of group tasks, whereas knowledge of the organization's rules is necessary (though not sufficient) to ensure order and workers' compliance. Only technical skills were measured in NASA-1, however.

3. Administration—B. *Fairness* is the affective requirement at the bottom level of leadership. Simple knowledge of the rules is not enough; they must be applied equitably with some recognition that in certain situations literal interpretations are inappropriate and individual context must be considered.

Katz and Kahn have warned against overemphasizing any particular leadership pattern, noting that the relative importance of any aspect depends upon the relation of the organization to its environment and also upon the level within the organizational hierarchy. We add that their three-level model treats middle-level and bottom-level leadership in drastically different ways. Although it is perhaps less apparent in their definitions than in their original discussion, they have not invested the third level of leadership with much influence. The essence of organizational leadership, as typically treated in the literature, resides in their middle level, interpolation. They seem to attribute to this level a larger sphere of activity than is assigned to either of the other two.

Although Katz and Kahn have discussed other aspects of leadership—like why it is necessary at all, different bases of power, and the importance of sharing the leadership function—their major contribution is this conceptualization of three processes of organizational leadership. To be sure, we may take issue with their particular descriptions of the patterns, but their approach nevertheless provides a significant elaboration of the theory of leadership functions in organizations. Furthermore, their suggestion of a cognitive and an affective requirement for each leadership pattern is a useful way to integrate their conceptualization with the two familiar dimensions of task orientation and socio-emotional orientation.

For our purposes, there is a minor drawback to their approach: It has not been tested empirically. Consequently our measures of their concepts are less certain than are those of the other conceptions of leadership; in the latter instances we were often able to use previously tested measures. Already we have noted that charisma has not been measured in our study; nor has "knowledge of organizational rules," part of the cognitive requirement for administration.

Measures of the Three Patterns

1. *Systemic perspective* (three-item index).[12] "How well does your supervisor understand the 'big picture' of what (the agency) is all about—does he see how (the agency's) mission relates to the social, economic, and political environment of the country? How good a job does your supervisor do at personally representing your work group in dealings with other groups in (the agency) or outside organizations?"

2. *Subsystem perspective* (four-item index).[13] "How good a job does your supervisor do at solving problems? How much influence does your supervisor have with his superiors and others up the line? To the extent that there are different view-points among those you work with, how successful is your supervisor in using these differences to get an effective end-product?"

3. *Integration of primary and secondary relationships* (five-item index). [14] "How successful has (the agency) been in getting you to meet its needs—for example, getting you to produce what they want, when they want it, in the manner they want? How good a job has (the agency) done at meeting your needs—for example, interesting work, adequate pay, a chance to use or develop your talents, or whatever is it that you want from your job?"

4. *Job knowledge* (single item).[15]

5. *Fairness* (three-item index). "How much confidence and

[12]This index included the item on institutional-leadership skills from the measures of skill mix.

[13] This index included the item on administrative skills from the measures of skill mix.

[14] This index included the items on human-relations skills from the measures of skill mix, as well as the items on encouraging teamwork and on maintaining high standards from the four-factor indexes of interaction facilitation and goal emphasis respectively.

[15] This item was the technical-skills item from the measures of skill mix.

trust do you have in your supervisor? To what extent does your present job provide an opportunity to work for competent, fair supervisors? To what extent does your present job provide an opportunity to be evaluated fairly in proportion to what you contribute?"

Likert's System IV

Just as Katz and Kahn treated leadership as part of a larger general organization theory, so has Likert in his system IV theory of organization; we shall consider primarily those aspects related to leadership. Likert presented his theory in 1961[16] and restated it in 1967.[17] He conceived of four different systems of management, which can be measured on such dimensions as character of motivational forces, communications processes, processes of interaction and influence, processes of decision-making and goal setting, and control. The system IV type of organization is the most advanced and, according to Likert, who drew heavily on research conducted at the Institute for Social Research, also the most effective.

Prime importance is attached to leadership as a causal variable. Three basic attributes of leadership are suggested: adherence to the principle of supportive relationships, high performance goals, and group methods of supervision. Likert has also mentioned technical and administrative skills, but he has not emphasised them as much as he has emphasised attributes; in fact, he has tended to accept them as given in the management situation.

Still another attribute emerges from Likert's discussion, though he has not discussed it separately: participation. Likert has usually combined it with the concept of group supervisory methods when discussing group decision-making. Participation may also occur, however, at the individual level. We shall therefore treat it separately from group methods.

Likert's conception has much in common with the other approaches, especially that of Bowers and Seashore, who have credited Likert with stimulating their own thinking. Likert's approach differs in its larger theoretical framework, which is both systemic in its emphasis and prescriptive in its overtones. He considers his basic leadership attributes as principles that

[16] Likert, *New Patterns of Management* (New York: McGraw-Hill, 1961).
[17] Likert, *The Human Organization*.

managers should practice in order to achieve more effective organizations. In both his books he has marshalled a great deal of evidence from organizational studies to demonstrate his arguments.

The *principle of supportive relationships* states that the supervisor—and all members of the organization for that matter—should behave toward each person so that the latter finds the interaction supportive in the light of his own background, expectations, and values and can use it to build and maintain his sense of personal worth and importance. This principle is virtually identical with the concept of support from the four-factor approach, and we measured the two in exactly the same manner.

The concept of setting, striving for, and creating enthusiasm for *high performance goals* is virtually identical with emphasis on goals in the four-factor approach. We measured them in exactly the same way.

Group methods of supervision include building work groups or teams throughout the organization. Although members of a particular work group operate as a group and engage in effective mutual interaction, they may belong to multiple groups. This principle is very similar to facilitation of interaction in the four-factor approach, but we have defined it as involving somewhat more work-oriented group behavior, specifically including group decision-making, and distinct from individual, "man-to-man" methods of supervision. System IV theory explicitly declares group methods in which the entire work group is involved in key decisions more appropriate than man-to-man methods in which the supervisor retains authority to make decisions and works with the individual members of the groups on an "as needed" basis.

As mentioned previously, the concept of *participation* is usually used in conjunction with that of group methods; in fact, system IV is called "participative-group" organization. We shall, however, treat participation as paralleling at the individual level the principle of group methods. It implies the greater involvement and influence of subordinates as individuals, rather than as a group, in matters affecting their work. Even though system IV does not distinguish participation from group methods, participation will be treated here as a full-fledged system IV concept.

System IV Measures

1. *Principle of supportive relationships.*[18]
2. *High performance goals.*[19]
3. *Group methods of supervision* (three-item index).[20] "Which of the following ways comes closest to describing how the important decisions are made in your division?"[21]
4. *Participation* (three-item index). "In solving job problems, does your supervisor generally try to get your ideas and opinions? To what extent do you feel that you, personally, can influence the activities and decisions of your supervisor on matters that are of concern to you? In carrying out the basic tasks of your job, does your supervisor supervise you closely or does he put you on your own?"

RELATIONSHIPS BETWEEN LEADERSHIP VARIABLES AND EFFECTIVENESS

Which of these many leadership variables are most highly related to effectiveness? Is supervisory behavior that is successful at one organizational level equally successful at another? How well do the data from NASA support the predictions of the various theories? Some answers to these questions are presented in Tables 6-1 to 6-4.

Skill-Mix Theory

Correlations between the skill-mix leadership variables and group effectiveness are presented in Table 6-1, in which significant positive relationships were predicted for all variables except institutional skills at the branch level.

The results indicate that at the division level human-rela-

[18] This measure was the index used to measure support in the four-factor approach.

[19] This measure was the index used to measure emphasis on goals in the four-factor approach.

[20] This measure included the item on encouraging teamwork from the index of interaction facilitation from the four-factor approach. This index differed from that one, however, in that it included an additional item, reflecting greater emphasis in system IV on decision-making in the group context. This particular item was designed to measure the decision-making and goal-setting characteristics (4f and 5a) specified by Likert, *The Human Organization,* pp. 21-22.

[21] Alternatives ranged from (1) "The division director makes the important decisions. He rarely asks for advice; he just gives orders" to (5) "A number of people are about equally involved. They usually get together and discuss the problem and agree on a solution."

TABLE 6-1 Correlations Between Leadership Variables and Effectiveness for Skill-Mix Theory, by Organizational Level

| | ORGANIZATIONAL LEVEL | | |
| | HIGHER (N = 12) | | LOWER (N = 28) |
SKILLS	OE*	RO†	RO†
Human relations	.58§	.64§	−.22
Technical	.62§	.06	−.04
Administrative	.61§	.42	−.14
Institutional	.48	.35	−.25

*Index of overall effectiveness from questionnaire.
†Rank-order measure of effectiveness from rankings by outside judges.
§Italics indicate that positive relationship was predicted; $p < .05$, two-tail.

tions, technical, and administrative skills were significantly related to effectiveness as measured by the questionnaire index. But only human-relations skills were also significantly related to the rank ordering, while the correlation between technical skills and the rank ordering was virtually zero ($r = .06$). Contrary to the prediction, institutional skills were not significantly related to either measure of effectiveness at the higher organizational level. At the lower organizational level none of the skill-mix variables was significantly related to effectiveness; in fact, the correlations at that level tended to be negative.

Among skill-mix variables, then, relationships with effectiveness were quite different at the higher and lower organizational levels. But this difference was not the one predicted by the theory (that technical and human-relations skills will be more important at lower levels and administrative and institutional skills more important at higher levels). No skills were related to effectiveness at the lower level, and institutional skill was the only one not significantly related to at least one of the two criteria at the higher level. The best predictor of effectiveness at the division level was the human-relations skills of the division director; it was significantly related to both the questionnaire and ranking measures. Technical and administrative skills were significantly related to the questionnaire measure only.

Four-Factor Theory

Table 6-2 presents the correlations of the variables from the four-factor theory with effectiveness. Four-factor theory

TABLE 6-2 Correlations Between Leadership Variables and Effectiveness for Four-Factor Theory, by Organizational Level

| | ORGANIZATIONAL LEVEL | | |
| | HIGHER (N = 12) | | LOWER (N = 28) |
FACTORS	OE*	RO†	RO†
Support	.61§	.41	−.21
Emphasis on Goals	.52**	.12	−.06
Facilitation of interaction	.27	.41	−.27
Facilitation of work	.73††	.51**	−.10

*Index of overall effectiveness from questionnaire.
†Rank-order measure of effectiveness from rankings by outside judges.
§Italics indicate that a positive relationship was predicted; $p < .05$, two-tail.
**In these correlations $p < .10$, two-tail.
††In this correlation $p < .01$, two-tail.

does not predict differently at the two organization levels.[22] Nevertheless, as in Table 6-1, no correlation at the branch level was significant; although quite low, they all tended to be negative. At the higher organizational level there were relationships with effectiveness, more significant with the questionnaire measure than with the ranking measure.

Support was significantly related to division effectiveness at the .05 level; goal emphasis tended to be related ($p < .10$). Neither of these two measures was significantly related to the rank ordering. Facilitation of interaction was not related to either the questionnaire or the ranking measure. Facilitation of work was, however, related to both measures, beyond the .01 level and beyond the .10 level of probability respectively.

In general, then, the four-factor variable most highly related to division effectiveness in our study was facilitation of work. Support and emphasis on goals followed in that order. Facilitation of interaction was least related to effectiveness. Finally, no four-factor variable was significantly related to effectiveness at the lower organizational level.

Three-Pattern Approach

Correlations between the three-pattern variables and effectiveness are presented in Table 6-3. As does the skill-mix

[22]Nor does it predict that the variables will be identically related at both levels. It treats levels of leadership in a different way altogether, as "peer" versus "managerial" leadership.

theory, the three-pattern approach assumes that the variables differ in importance according to organizational level. But note that only systemic perspective is not expected to have a significant positive relationship with effectiveness at the lower level. Otherwise the variables are listed in the order of their predicted importance for the higher organizational level.

Once again the results showed no significant relationship with effectiveness at the branch level. At the division level all the variables except systemic perspective were significantly related to the questionnaire measure of effectiveness. In addition, subsystem perspective and integration tended ($p < .10$) to be related to the rank ordering. Job knowledge was not at all related to the rank ordering ($r = .06$). Fairness was significantly related only to the questionnaire measure of effectiveness.

Among the three-pattern variables subsystem perspective and integration were the most related to division effectiveness and systemic perspective the least; job knowledge and fairness fell between. Strictly speaking, three-pattern theory predicts that systemic perspective should be more important at the higher level than it appears to have been in our study. Otherwise the relative strength of relationships with effectiveness at the division level was about as expected, with subsystem perspective and integration somewhat more important than job

TABLE 6-3 *Correlations Between Leadership Variables and Effectiveness for Three-Pattern Theory, by Organizational Level*

| | ORGANIZATIONAL LEVEL | | |
| | HIGHER ($N = 12$) | | LOWER ($N = 28$) |
THREE-PATTERN REQUIREMENTS	OE*	RO†	RO†
Systemic perspective	.49§	.40	−.26
Subsystem perspective	.72**	.50††	−.16
Integration	.70§§	.51††	−.13
Job knowledge	.62§§	.06	−.04
Fairness	.59§§	.37	−.19

*Index of overall effectiveness from questionnaire.
†Rank-order measure of effectiveness from rankings by outside judges.
§Italics indicate that a positive relationship was predicted.
**In this correlation $p < .01$, two-tail.
††In these correlations $p < .10$, two-tail.
§§In these correlations $p < .05$, two-tail.

knowledge and fairness. The lack of significant relationships with effectiveness, especially for job knowledge and fairness at the lower organization level, was not expected.

System IV

Table 6-4 presents the correlations between system IV leadership variables and effectiveness. As the first two system IV variables are identical with the first two four-factor variables, the top half of Table 6-4 is the same as the top half of Table 6-2. Again predictions for the two organizational levels were not differentiated.

Neither of the two new variables presented in Table 6-4 was significantly related to effectiveness. Regardless of organizational level and of the measure of effectiveness used, group methods and participation were not related significantly to group effectiveness.

The system IV leadership variable most related to division effectiveness was supportive relationships. High performance goals tended ($p < .10$) to be related, but group methods and participation did not. None of the four variables was related to the ranking of effectiveness; system IV seems slightly less useful in this respect than the other theories do, for at least one variable in each of the latter was related to ranking of effectiveness at the .10 level or better. System IV did share with the other theories its failure to reveal any significant relationships with effectiveness at the branch level.

TABLE 6-4 Correlations Between Leadership Variables and Effectiveness for System IV Theory, by Organizational Level

| | ORGANIZATIONAL LEVEL | | |
| | HIGHER ($N = 12$) | | LOWER ($N = 28$) |
LEADERSHIP VARIABLES	OE*	RO†	RO†
Supportive relationships	.61§	.41	−.21
High performance goals	.52**	.12	−.06
Group methods	.05	.33	−.24
Participation	.44	.16	−.15

*Index of overall effectiveness from questionnaire.
†Rank-order measure of effectiveness from rankings by outside judges.
§Italics indicate that a positive relationship was predicted; $p < .05$, two-tail.
**In this correlation $p < .10$, two-tail.

Summary

The most obvious and consistent finding among the correlations between all these leadership variables and group effectiveness was that none of the former was significantly
related to effectiveness at the lower organizational level. Possible reasons for this finding will be discussed later.

At the division level leadership variables were more often
related to the questionnaire measure of effectiveness than to
the ranking measure. Each theory included at least one variable related to this measure at the .05 level. The three-pattern
variables were slightly more able to predict effectiveness,
whereas system IV variables were slightly less. Skill mix
and four-factor variables lay about equally between in predictive power.

Human-relations skills were the only variable correlated
at the .05 level with both the ranking and the questionnaire
measures. Facilitation of work, subsystem perspective, and integration tended to have slightly higher correlations (in the low
.70s) with effectiveness, whereas institutional skills, systemic perspective, facilitation of interaction, group methods, and participation showed no significant relationships. Goal emphasis and high performance goals were related to effectiveness
at only the .10 probability level. How the variables from each
theory worked together to predict effectiveness is the topic of
the next section, in which we shall use multiple-regression
analysis.

MULTIPLE-REGRESSION ANALYSES FOR EACH THEORETICAL APPROACH TO PREDICTING EFFECTIVENESS

The correlations between leadership variables and effectiveness
presented in Tables 6-1 to 6-4 do not provide a very precise
overall picture of how well each theory accounts for effective
performance. They do not indicate how relationships among
the variables for each theory affect predictions of effectiveness.
For example, three of the four correlations between skill-mix
variables and the index of overall effectiveness were significant
(see Table 6-1). Because of correlations among the variables
themselves, however, the correlations in Table 6-1 cannot
be simply added together to determine the overall predictability of the skill-mix model. Multiple-regression analysis is
useful to us here because it tells us how much each variable
is contributing to the variance of the effectiveness measures

and does it in a way that eliminates the double counting of variance that two variables may share jointly with effectiveness.

Tables 6-5 to 6-8 present the results of each of the theories predicting effectiveness. Readers are reminded that multiple Rs, because they involve more variables, lose more degrees of freedom and consequently must be considerably higher than simple rs in order to be statistically significant. When there are five variables (four leadership measures and the index of effectiveness) the R for division data must be .838 to be significant at the .05 level, two-tail. For branch data the R must be .572. The reader is further reminded that, despite these increased standards of significance, the obtained R always tends to be an inflated estimate of the populations R, particularly when the sample N is low, as it is here, for it capitalizes on chance errors in the data that will be different in other sets of data. The Rs obtained in the present study should therefore be considered as indications of how well the theories accounted for effectiveness only in our data and not necessarily in other sets of data as well.

Skill-Mix Theory

Table 6-5 presents the beta weights and multiple Rs for skill-mix variables and effectiveness at higher and lower organizational levels. Once again, the questionnaire index and rank ordering were used at the division level, but only rank ordering was used at the branch level. Note that the variables have been listed in order of their *predicted* importance for each level.

At the branch level the R was rather small and not significant. This finding tends to confirm the results in Table 6-1, and indicates that even when the skills were considered together they were not related significantly to effectiveness at the lower organizational level. But, the relationship with effectiveness at the upper level, measured in the same way, is rather strong and statistically significant. The skill-mix variables, taken together, predict rankings of effectiveness at the division level rather well, accounting for 72 percent of the variance in the ranking scores.

The effectiveness scores on the questionnaire index were predicted less accurately than were the rankings, which is somewhat surprising considering that the reverse was true in Table

TABLE 6-5 Multiple-Regression Analysis of Leadership Variables and Effectiveness for Skill-Mix Theory, by Organizational Level

	HIGHER LEVEL (N = 12)			LOWER LEVEL (N = 28)	
		BETA			BETA
SKILLS*	OE†	RO§	SKILLS*		RO§
Institutional	.082	.602	Technical		.469
Administrative	.223	.193	Human relations		−.421
Human relations	.206	.764	Administrative		.038
Technical	.305	−.920	Institutional		−.281
	R = .696	.848**		R =	.373
	R^2 = .484	.719		R^2 =	.139

*In order of greatest *predicted* importance for each level.
†Index of overall effectiveness from questionnaire.
§Rank-order measure of effectiveness from rankings by outside judges.
**In this correlation $p < .05$, two-tail.

6-1. Although almost half the variance in effectiveness on this index was accounted for by the skill-mix variables, the R of .696 failed to reach the .05 probability level. This failure may seem incongruous, considering that the questionnaire score was predicted significantly by measures of three of the four skills in Table 6-1. But this incongruity reveals one of the virtues of multiple-regression analysis. The highest correlation in this study was the .62 between technical skills and the questionnaire index (see Table 6-1). This correlation was increased only negligibly when other variables were added to the prediction equation because the skills shared some common variance with the questionnaire index.

Note that the beta weights for the ranking criterion were quite different from those for the questionnaire criterion. Apparently the common variance among the four skills was not also shared with the ranking, as it was with the questionnaire index. This difference reflects the greater independence of the ranking measure. Technical skill was the most influential variable in predicting the questionnaire index, whereas human-relations skill was most influential in predicting ranking.

The beta weight for technical skills in predicting ranking was negative and quite high ($−.920$), suggesting that after the common variance of technical and other skills has been taken into account, the former were related negatively to effectiveness as measured by ranking. Technical skills were thus a suppressor variable reducing the effects of other variables on effectiveness.

The role of technical skills in predicting effectiveness rankings was not, however, quite as dramatic as the figure $-.920$ at first suggests. The appropriate beta weight was used to adjust the correlation of each variable with the criterion of effectiveness in solving the regression equation for R^2. As technical skills were correlated only $r = .06$ with ranking (see Table 6-1), that actually accounted for less than 6 percent of the total predicted variance in ranking. That is, when they were combined with human-relations, administrative, and institutional skills, technical skills made a very small contribution to prediction of rankings of division effectiveness in our study.

Nevertheless, the beta weight was negative, and why it was is not at all clear. One of the problems with using multiple-regression analysis is that it occasionally produces findings that are quite unexpected and difficult to understand in the light of data obtained from more elementary statistical methods. In this instance there appears to have been some slight variance in the ranking measure not related to the other three skills but related negatively to a slight variance in the technical skills that was also not related to the other three skills.

In summary, multiple-regression analysis indicated that the skill-mix variables, taken together, accounted rather well for effectiveness rankings at the division level but not at the branch level. But multiple correlation really was unnecessary for the questionnaire measure, as all the significant variance could be accounted for by the simple r between technical skills and the questionnaire index. In contrast to overall skill-mix predictions, correlations of technical skills with the questionnaire index and of human-relations skills with ranking contributed the most to accounting for effectiveness at the higher organizational levels.

Four-Factor Theory

Results of the multiple-regression analyses for four-factor theory and effectiveness are presented in Table 6-6. At the lower organizational level R was low and not significant. The same was true at the upper level for the ranking criterion of effectiveness. Both these results might have been suspected on the basis of the results of simple correlations between four-factor variables and ranking shown in Table 6-2. But the R with the questionnaire index was high and significant; four-

TABLE 6-6 Multiple-Regression Analysis of Leadership Variables and Effectiveness
for Four-Factor Theory, by Organizational Level

	HIGHER LEVEL (N = 12)			LOWER LEVEL (N = 28)	
	BETA				BETA
FACTORS*	OE†	RO§	FACTORS*		RO§
Support	.409	.066	Support		−.361
Emphasis on goals	.301	−.091	Emphasis on goals		.682
Facilitation of interaction	−.351	.116	Facilitation of interaction		−.560
Facilitation of work	.549	.429	Facilitation of work		−.042
R =	.845**	.530		R =	.431
R² =	.714	.281		R² =	.186

*Four-factor variables are not ordered in terms of strength of their relation-
ships with effectiveness, nor does the theory make different predictions for different
organizational levels.
† Index of overall effectiveness from questionnaire.
§ Rank-order measure of effectiveness from rankings by outside judges.
**In this correlation $p < .05$, two-tail.

factor variables accounted for 71 percent of the variance in
questionnaire effectiveness for the divisions.

Although four-factor theory makes no specific predictions about how its variables will be related to effectiveness,
we note that facilitation of work with a beta weight of .549
(and an r with the questionnaire index of .73; see Table 6-2),
clearly contributed most to accounting for effectiveness. In
fact, comparison between r of .73 for facilitation of work with
questionnaire effectiveness and the R of .845 in Table 6-6 indicates that the other three four-factor variables added only 11
points to the correlation.

There was also a negative beta weight, −.351, for facilitation of interaction, but, as this variable was correlated only
.27 with the questionnaire index, its influence in the regression
equation was small. Nevertheless the minus sign did indicate
that when the common variance between facilitation of interaction and the other variables was held constant, the former
was negatively related to the index of effectiveness, suggesting
that "pure interaction facilitation" behavior by the supervisor
reduces, rather than increases, the effectiveness of his group.

In summary, four-factor theory accounted for the index
of effectiveness quite well but not for the ranking of effectiveness. The most influential predictor among the four-factor
variables was facilitation of work.

Three-Pattern Approach

Beta weights and multiple Rs for three-pattern variables and effectiveness are presented in Table 6-7. The variables have been listed in the order of their predicted importance for each level. Only the R for rankings of effectiveness at the division level was significant. In view of earlier results the absence of a significant R at the branch level is not surprising. The R for the questionnaire index was not significant because the latter was already predicted quite well by subsystem perspective alone (see Table 6-3). Because of interrelations among the three-pattern variables, adding them to the prediction equation contributed very little new variance.

TABLE 6-7 *Multiple-Regression Analysis of Leadership Variables and Effectiveness for Three-Pattern Theory, by Organizational Level*

	HIGHER LEVEL (N = 12)			LOWER LEVEL (N = 28)	
	BETA				BETA
VARIABLES*	OE†	RO§	VARIABLES*		RO§
Systemic perspective	.014	.568	Subsystem perspective		.093
Subsystem perspective	.449	.693	Integration		−.217
Integration	.711	1.025	Job knowledge		.518
Job knowledge	.107	−1.323	Fairness		−.128
Fairness	−.496	− .445	Systemic perspective		−.465
R =	.779	.919**		R =	.368
R^2 =	.606	.844		R^2 =	.135

*In order of greatest *predicted* importance for each level.
†Index of overall effectiveness from questionnaire.
§Rank-order measure of effectiveness from rankings by outside judges.
**In this correlation $p < .05$, two-tail.

The R for ranking at the division level was .919, indicating that three-pattern variables accounted for 84 percent of the variance in effectiveness rankings for divisions. Readers are reminded that, although the multiple correlation was indeed high, it was inflated, particularly in a sample as small as the present one and with the five predictors involved in the three-pattern approach. To be significant at the .05 probability level, with an N of twelve and six variables in the regression equation, the R would have had to be .886.

The beta weights indicated that, when all variables were combined, integration was dominant in accounting for ranking effectiveness. The weight for job knowledge was also high (and negative), but we recall that job knowledge was measured by technical skills. In our discussion of the multiple-regression analysis of skill-mix theory we noted that, because of the low r (.06) between technical skills and ranking, the influence of the former was not nearly as great as it seemed at first. The same is true in the current instance.

A more potent negative relationship was revealed in analysis of fairness, which was correlated .37 with ranking (see Table 6-3) and had a beta weight of $-.445$. When the common variance of fairness and the other three-pattern variables was held constant, fairness contributed negatively to ranking effectiveness. But it was the last variable to enter into the prediction when stepwise regression procedure was used, and it contributed only negligibly to the multiple R. The information presented in Table 6-7 thus does not tell quite the entire story. This instance demonstrates some complexities of multiple-regression analyses that are better left for exploration in another study. Our purpose here is merely to note the general usefulness of each approach in accounting for effectiveness as measured by our data, to point out which variables are dominant, and to highlight important departures from expectations.

In this respect the multiple-regression analyses results for the three-pattern approach may be summarized this way: The Rs for the lower organizational level and for the questionnaire index at the upper level were not significant; in the latter instance multiple correlation was really not necessary to predict effectiveness, for subsystem perspective could do it satisfactorily alone.[23] At the upper organizational level the three-pattern approach accounted for a high proportion of ranking effectiveness; integration was the dominant predictor.

System IV

Results for the final series of multiple regressions, involving system IV and effectiveness, are presented in Table 6-8. Once again the R for the branch level was low and not significant. In fact, the Rs at the higher organizational level were both so close to the .05 level that it seems foolish to con-

[23] Strictly speaking, it could not really do the job alone. The simple r between subsystem perspective and the questionnaire index included variance shared with the other variables; in the regression analysis, however, this variation was not duplicated when the other variables entered the equation.

clude that system IV variables together were not related to effectiveness at the division level. On one hand, the lack of significance seems to reflect the generally lower success of system IV variables in predicing effectiveness (see Table 6-4). On the other hand, the Rs for the division level in Table 6-8 show how predictive success can be increased by combining variables. Improvement was especially strong for the ranking criterion, whose multiple R was 40 correlation points higher than the highest single correlation in Table 6-4. Nevertheless, because of the small size of the sample and the upward bias of R, our discussion must be rather tentative.

TABLE 6-8 Multiple-Regression Analysis of Leadership Variables and Effectiveness for System IV Theory, by Organizational Level

	HIGHER LEVEL ($N = 12$)			LOWER LEVEL ($N = 28$)	
		BETA			BETA
VARIABLES*	OE†	RO§	VARIABLES*		RO§
Supportive relationships	1.039	1.447	Supportive relationships		− .418
High performance goals	.602	.486	High performance goals		.646
Group methods	.131	.910	Group methods		.566
Participation	− .633	−1.699	Participation		.092
$R^{**} =$	.823	.830		$R =$	.411
$R^2 =$	.678	.690		$R^2 =$	.169

*System IV concepts are not ordered in terms of the strength of their relationships with effectiveness, nor does the theory make different predictions for different organizational levels.

†Index of overall effectiveness from questionnaire.

§Rank-order measure of effectiveness from rankings by outside judges.

**R necessary for $p < .05$ with five variables and $N = 12$ is .838.

Actually, what happened to the R for the questionnaire index is similar to what happened in some situations discussed previously. One variable, supportive relationships, predicted overall effectiveness significantly ($r = .61$, Table 6-4). Adding more variables to the equation did increase the variance accounted for, but it also decreased the degrees of freedom; the resulting R was thus not significant.

Supportive relationships were also the dominant variable in predicting ranking effectiveness. Participation had a fairly important negative weight in both predictions. In preliminary analyses we discovered that participation was quite strongly related to supportive relationships and, to a lesser extent, also to high performance goals and group methods. It appears that, when the variance that it shared with the other system IV variables was held constant, its unique contribution to the correlation with effectiveness was negative. When participation was allowed to interact freely with the other system IV variables, as in Table 6-4, its contribution was positive.

In the stepwise regression for ranking, participation appeared second, after supportive relationships. Its beta weight at that point was $-.552$, and R was .516. When high performance goals were added in the third step, R became .713, and the beta weight for participation jumped to -1.205. Results for the fourth and final step can be seen in Table 6-8. This curious sequence seems worthy of note. Apparently "pure participation," devoid of a rather substantial built-in support component, contributed negatively to effectiveness, especially when high performance goals and group methods were also included. An oversimple explanation is that engaging in participation without also being supportive does not increase effectiveness and even tends to reduce it. But the evidence for this conclusion is too tenuous for us to state it with certainty.

In summary, multiple-regression analysis for system IV and effectiveness showed no significant Rs, but at the division level the Rs were sizable and extremely close to significance for both the questionnaire and ranking measures of effectiveness. Supportive relationships were the dominant predictor and for the questionnaire index their simple r with effectiveness was significant. Participation played a negative part in the multiple correlations with effectiveness.

This entire section on multiple-regression analysis for each leadership theory and effectiveness has demonstrated that none of the approaches predicted effectiveness at the lower organizational level but that all did for one or the other of the two criteria at the division level. System IV accounted for both effectiveness measures about equally but not quite at the .05 level of significance. The skill-mix and three-pattern approaches accounted for rankings significantly but not for the questionnaire measures. The reverse was true of the four-factor theory. Most often the multiple Rs failed to reach significance because additional variables beyond the highest single predictor failed to add new variance of any consequence. A few variables seemed to contribute negatively to effectiveness, though their influence was usually slight. Comparing results from the four theories suggests that all accounted about equally well for effective division performance in our data.

ZERO-ORDER CORRELATIONS
BETWEEN LEADERSHIP AND EFFECTIVENESS

The correlations in Tables 6-1 to 6-4 reveal a wide range in the extent to which leadership variables were related to organizational effectiveness. Furthermore, these correlations were quite different for the two organizational levels; they were frequently of moderate size and statistically significant at the division level but uniformly low, negative, and not significant at the branch level. At the division level they tended to be higher for the index measure than for the ranking measure. Possible reasons for these differences in level and criterion will be discussed later. For the present we shall discuss only data from the division level.

In general, there was no one leadership variable that stood out as an especially good predictor of effectiveness, but some variables seemed slightly more predictive and others slightly less.

Among skill-mix variables, human-relations skills were the only ones significantly related to both criteria of effectiveness at the division level. Institutional skills were not significantly related to either effectiveness measure. In theory, the findings should have been just the reverse.

Apparently a division director's ability to work well with people was an important aspect of effectiveness, as viewed both by people in the division and by people outside. This finding suggests that in the kind of administrative organization studied by us—largely service organizations designed to help and to control other work units, through the development of programs and procedures — skills in working with others may be of great importance.

The insignificant relationship of institutional skills to division effectiveness may indicate that division directors do not occupy a high enough level in the larger organization for their institutional skills to have much importance. This explanation seems unlikely, however. Although it is true that there are several managerial levels above them, division directors do propose policy for the agency as a whole (but within their functional areas) and coordinate programs both within their own agencies and with other Federal agencies.

Among four-factor variables, facilitation of work was the best predictor of division effectiveness for both criteria. Support and emphasis on goals were also related but not to both criteria. It appears that the technical and administrative behavior of division directors contributes in important ways to division effectiveness. Support also contributes to effectiveness, no doubt for the same reasons as do human-relations skills. But the correlation between outside effectiveness rankings and support did not reach significance, whereas that between human-relations skills and such rankings did. This failure may reflect a tendency for supportive behavior to be more "internally oriented," whereas human-relations skills may be equally relevant inside and outside the division.[24]

Facilitation of interaction was the four-factor variable least related to division effectiveness; it was not related to either measure. Apparently developing and working with subordinates in groups did not contribute to division effectiveness, perhaps because branches to some extent worked independently of one another. Thus for many purposes it was neither useful nor essential for the division director to work with his branch chiefs on a group basis. It is also possible that supervisors lacked the extra skills necessary for working at the group level and that, even when facilitation of interaction was appropriate and attempted, it was not accomplished very well.

Results for system IV variables were basically the same as those for four-factor variables and need not be repeated here. The one difference was that facilitation of work, the best predictor in four-factor theory, was not included among system IV variables in our study. The fourth system IV variable was participation. As it was not significantly related to effectiveness, system IV variables predicted effectiveness less well overall than did the variables from other theories in our study. It is possible that the supportive-behavior component of participation contributed to effectiveness, whereas participation by itself did not.

The three-pattern variables most highly related to effectiveness were subsystem perspective and integration; both

[24] Division directors' human-relations skills may be more visible to outsiders, beside contributing more to division effectiveness.

incorporated the major features of facilitation of work and human-relations skills respectively. Their contributions to effectiveness therefore most likely resulted from the same sources as did those of facilitation of work and human-relations skills. Systematic perspective failed, as did institutional skills, to be significantly related to effectiveness, whereas job knowledge and fairness were as significantly related to the index measure, as were technical skills and support respectively. Thus the three-pattern variables were related to effectiveness just as all the other variables were, with no unique contributions.

Before discussing the absence of significant relationships between leadership and effectiveness at the branch level, we note once again the tendency for correlations with the questionnaire index to be higher and significant more often than were those with the ranking measure. As we remarked earlier, this difference no doubt reflected the greater independence of the ranking measure. As division ranking was significantly predicted both by individual leadership variables and by multiple Rs, however, we do not attribute the successful correlations with the index solely to the potential bias inherent in using the questionnaire measure. Organization studies frequently use correlations between independent and dependent variables derived from the same instrument. Although this efficiency does not render the procedure desirable, it is often the only one available. Indeed we were fortunate in our analysis of leadership to have two measures that made it possible to judge how serious the bias was. It appears to have been not very serious, but a certain amount of caution is necessary in interpreting correlations with index effectiveness.

BRANCH LEADERSHIP AND EFFECTIVENESS

Just as the data show clear and significant relationships between division leadership and division effectiveness, they show a clear absence of any relationship between branch leadership and branch effectiveness. Why? The failure to find such relationships may result from any of several factors. One possibility is that the ranking criterion is not very appropriate at that level. As the same measure was related to leadership at the division level, however, and, as its reliability at the branch level was adequate though not high (.63), it is unlikely that the criterion itself was the sole source of the problem. It could be that the *overall* effectiveness measure was less relevant at the branch level than at the division level. Differences in various areas of performance may become blurred at higher organizational levels, whereas at lower levels they remain sharper; supervisory behavior may be related to some subcriteria of the ranking criterion but not to others. Perhaps there was enough error in the rankings of branch effectiveness and in the descriptions of branch leadership to yield a net-zero relationship when the two measures were correlated.

It is quite possible, of course, that branch leadership is simply not related to branch effectiveness. Indeed, Katz and Kahn have suggested that lower-level organizational leadership may have little effect upon group performance, primarily because it is often devoid of the influence necessary to affect what is done or how it is done in the branch.[25] The branch chiefs in our study, however, occupied more important positions than did Katz and Kahn's bottom-level leaders. Furthermore, there were evident no technological factors that might have produced a leveling effect on the productivity of the branches.[26]

Another possibility is that effectiveness of branches, as subunits of divisions, cannot be considered independently of division effectiveness—or the reverse. Indeed, we hardly expect the effectiveness of a division to be unrelated to that of the branches that compose it. Nor do we necessarily expect effectiveness to be identical at both levels. Not all division work is done in branches; some divisions have no branches, and some divisions have branches not separated in our data (usually because of size). Furthermore, effectiveness scores for branches often varied widely within the same division. Nevertheless, on the average, branch effectiveness and division effectiveness were related and quite closely at that. For the seven divisions with branches in our study, the correlation between the average ranking scores for branches within a division and the independently obtained ranking scores for the divisions as wholes was .86.

This finding still does not entirely explain the differences in correlations between leadership and effectiveness at the two

[25] Katz and Kahn, *op. cit.*

[26] A more likely constraining influence than technology is bureaucratic procedures. Branch chiefs may be hemmed in by the rules, regulations, and prescribed procedures that frequently govern job performance at the bottom levels of large bureaucracies, especially in the federal government.

organizational levels. In fact, on this basis we might just as easily expect to find significant correlations at the branch level, rather than at the division level. But, as division leadership was not correlated with branch effectiveness, whereas division and branch effectiveness were related, we must now examine two additional analyses.

First, we should see whether or not division leadership was related to branch leadership; if it was not, we might then look at relationships between branch leadership and branch effectiveness within divisions, thus holding constant division influence on branch effectiveness scores. Analyses of variance by branch within divisions revealed significant differences among leadership scores for branches from the same division. Furthermore, "average branch leadership" for each division was not correlated with division leadership across the seven divisions that had branches. There was no relationship between the behavior of the division director and that of the branch chiefs.

Our second analysis correlated branch leadership scores with branch effectiveness scores within divisions. Unfortunately there were only two divisions with enough branches to warrant this analysis, and even then there were small Ns (6 and 7 respectively). We found no significant relationship between supervisory behavior by branch chiefs and branch effectiveness in these two divisions. Correlations were both positive and negative with no apparent pattern; most were quite low. Branch leadership appeared unrelated to branch effectiveness.

We are forced to conclude that the data offer no clear explanations of why there were no significant relationships between supervisory behavior of branch chiefs and branch effectiveness. It appears that all the reasons discussed are possible but that none stands out as the answer.

MULTIPLE-REGRESSION ANALYSES FOR EACH THEORETICAL APPROACH PREDICTING TO EFFECTIVENESS

Our final discussion involves the general question of which leadership theory as a whole best accounts for effectiveness. The answer can be found in the multiple-regression analyses summarized in Tables 6-5 to 6-8. All the theories scored about equally, each accounting for one or the other of the division criteria satisfactorily but none predicting branch effectiveness adequately.

But Tables 6-5 to 6-8 also suggest that these theories all have an unnecessary component—redundancy. In several instances we found that multiple Rs with effectiveness were not much higher than were the highest simple rs. In fact, on two occasions additional variables added so little new variance that the resulting R was not significant even though the highest r had been, which suggests that leadership variables rapidly reach their maximum predictive power. Perhaps if they differed from one another more they would be more useful, when taken together, in accounting for effectiveness.

A good example of this problem is the results for system IV variables, especially in predicting division rankings. The highest single r between a system IV variable (supportive relationships) and ranking was .41. Yet the multiple R was .83. Each new variable contributed 10 to 20 correlation points to R, primarily because our system IV variables were somewhat less interrelated than were the variables for the other theories. In contrast, the multiple R for the skill-mix variables predicting the questionnaire index (see Table 6-5) was .696, yet technical skills by themselves were correlated .62 with the index (see Table 6-1), indicating that the other three skills added only 7 points to the correlation. In fact, the first six of these seven additional points were contributed by human-relations skills. The other two skills contributed virtually nothing to the prediction.

We also saw in the system IV multiple correlations an example of the kind of unexpected findings that multiple-regression analyses often reveal. Specifically, participation contributed negatively, as indicated by its negative beta weight, to the prediction of effectiveness, despite its positive r with effectiveness. Apparently this r resulted from the interaction between participation and other system IV variables. The multiple correlation, by holding constant the interrelation among the "independent" variables, [27] exposed relationships that would otherwise have remained hidden. Except for the beta weight of participation, however, the negative beta weights that occured in our study made negligible contributions to total predictions.

[27] Because of their interrelations our leadership variables were often not "independent." Of the system IV variables participation was significantly related to both supportive relationships and group methods.

As Rs, particularly those based on small samples, tend to be inflated, we shall spare ourselves an extended discussion of the results of multiple-regression analyses and shall conclude simply that there are no real differences in the power of these four leadership theories to predict effectiveness; they all include some redundancy among their leadership variables, but in general they are all equally useful at the division level and equally useless at the branch level.

CONCLUSIONS

Correlations between leadership and effectiveness revealed that all theories have some predictive power. Division effectiveness could be predicted fairly well from the supervisory behavior of the division director. In skill-mix theory the best predictor of overall effectiveness ratings and rankings was human-relations skills, in four-factor theory facilitation of work, in three-pattern theory subsystem perspective and integration, and in system IV theory, supportive relationships. All these predictors belong to the familiar "task orientation" and "group maintenance" functions of leadership. Multiple-regression analyses revealed that the theories were about equally useful in accounting for effectiveness at the division level, though frequently the inclusion of variables beyond the single highest predictor added little new variance to the prediction. None of the leadership variables was related to effectiveness at the lower organizational level, perhaps because of weaknesses in the data at that level or perhaps for other reasons. Leadership thus had considerable, significant, but definitely limited relationships to organizational effectiveness. Other variables like motivation, satisfaction, technology, coordination, communication, and so on must be considered along with leadership in order to understand organizational effectiveness.

7
Leadership Styles, Situations, and Organizational Effectiveness

Three major types of leadership theory have been designed by social psychologists for application to large organizations: the democratic, multifactor, and situational theories. Democratic leadership theories are the oldest and, though they take many forms, there is a core of ideas common to them all. It is assumed that democratic leadership practices generate higher morale and job satisfaction among subordinates. Some advocates go father and assume that these practices also produce better work performance.[1] The democratic supervisor is expected to maintain open communications with his subordinates, discussing work changes, listening to their ideas about work problems, and expressing appreciation of their efforts.[2]

Empirical tests of these theories have not produced unqualified confirmation. No necessary relationship between morale and job performance or between democratic supervisory techniques and job performance has been found. Other studies[3] have identified a series of intervening variables—

[1]F. Roethlisberger and W. Dickson, *Management and the Worker* (Cambridge, Mass.: Harvard University Press, 1947), pp. 583 *et passim;* K. Lewin, R. Lippitt, and R. White, "Patterns of Aggressive Behavior in Experimentally Created Climates," *Journal of Social Psychology* 10 (1939): 271-299; Lewin, "Group Decision-Making and Social Change," in *Readings in Social Psychology,* ed. T. Newcomb and E. Hartley (New York: Holt, 1947), pp. 330-344; L. Coch and John R. P. French, Jr., "Overcoming Resistance to Change," in *Group Dynamics,* ed. Dorwin Cartwright and Alvin Zander (New York: Harper & Row, 1956), pp. 257-279; and Elton Mayo, *The Human Problems of an Industrial Civilization,* 2nd ed. (New York: Macmillan, 1945), p. 172.

[2]Norman Maier, *Principles of Human Relations: Applications to Management,* (New York: Wiley, 1952), pp. 5-7.

[3] W. Haythorn, "The Effects of Varying Compositions of Authoritarian and Equalitarian Leaders and Followers," *Readings in Social Psychology,* 3rd

the personalities of work-group members, the legitimacy of different leadership patterns, and the nature of the work—that suggest limits to the applicability of the democratic approach. Data from the study of ten Michigan hospitals reflect these limitations of democratic theory. Table 7-1 shows that the measures of democratic supervision were not related in the expected positive direction to hospital effectiveness.

From their reviews of attempts to evaluate democratic-leadership theory, many social scientists concluded that a fundamental reappraisal of leadership theory, particularly as related to the effectiveness of work groups, was necessary. This reappraisal led to the development of multifactor theories. In the earliest stages of this development some two-factor theories were proposed.[4] Although different social scientists gave the factors different names, the contents were quite similar. One factor, which we shall call the "task factor," included those activities of leaders, group members, or both intended to implement work objectives: setting standards, scheduling, coordinating, rewarding, and so on. The second factor included activities designed to integrate the group socioemotionally: showing appreciation and support, reducing tension, showing concern for personal needs of individual workers, and so on. This factor is variously called "expressive," "socioemotional," or "consideration structure."

D. Anthony Butterfield[5] has shown that studies of two-

ed., ed. E. Maccoby, T. Newcomb, and E. Hartley (New York: Holt, Rinehart and Winston, 1958), pp. 511-521; Victor Vroom, *Some Personality Determinants of the Effects of Participation* (Englewood Cliffs, N.J.: Prentice-Hall, 1960); Stuart Adams, "Status Congruency as a Variable in Small Group Performance," *Social Forces* 7 (October 1953): 16-22; and G. E. Swanson," The Effectiveness of Decision-Making Groups," *Adult Leadership* 8 (June 1959): 48-52.

[4] R. F. Bales, "Task Roles and Social Roles in Problem-Solving Groups," in *Readings in Social Psychology*, 3rd ed., ed. E. Maccoby, T. M. Newcomb, and E. L. Hartley (New York: Holt, Rinehart and Winston, 1958), pp. 437-447; P. E. Slater, "Role Differentiation in Small Groups," in *Small Groups: Studies in Social Interaction*, ed. A. P. Hare, E. F. Borgatta, and Bales, (New York: Knopf, 1955), pp. 498-515; A. W. Halpin, "The Leadership Behavior and Combat Performance of Airplane Commanders," *Journal of Abnormal and Social Psychology* 49 (1954): 15-22; E. A. Fleishman, E. F. Harris, and H. E. Burtt, *Leadership and Supervision in Industry* (Ohio State University, Bureau of Educational Research Monograph #33, 1955); and J. K. Hemphill, "Leadership Behavior Associated with the Administrative Reputations of College Departments, *Journal of Educational Psychology* 46 (1955): 385-402.

[5] D. A. Butterfield, "Supervisory Behavior and Effectiveness: A Review of Empirical Research and Current Thinking" (unpublished ms., Institute for Social Research, The University of Michigan, 1967).

TABLE 7-1 *Relationships Between Measures of Supervisory Skills and Measures of Organizational Effectiveness**

MEASURES OF SUPERVISORY SKILLS	MEASURES OF ORGANIZATIONAL EFFECTIVENESS			
	OVERALL QUALITY OF PATIENT CARE	PREVALENCE OF ADAPTATION	PROMPTNESS OF ADAPTATION	FLEXIBILITY
Supervisor's ability to deal with people	−.73	.28	.13	−.18
Frequency with which employees feel free to discuss personal problems with superiors	−.26	.21	.16	−.18
Frequency with which supervisor expresses appreciation of employee performance	−.12	.01	−.05	−.35
Degree to which subordinate is sure what his supervisor thinks of his work	.03	−.03	.06	−.06
Frequency with which supervisor announces work changes in advance	−.11	.36	−.07	−.56
Frequency with which supervisor asks employee's opinions about work problem	.03	.38	−.19	−.22
Ease of communicating ideas about job changes to supervisor	.11	.46	.11	−.39
Degree to which supervisor understands people at lower levels	.17	.56	.48	−.30

*Spearman rank-order correlations were used. The total sample was ten hospitals, with an average of n of 120 respondents per hospital; r_s = .56 is therefore significant at the .05 level and r_s = .75 at the .01 level.

factor theory also produced conflicting results. In some settings both factors were related to group effectiveness, whereas in others neither was and in still others only one was related to effectiveness in the expected direction. This confusion adds a dimension to Butterfield's basic finding in Chapter 6 of this book that multifactor theories were no more useful than were two-factor theories in predicting organizational effectiveness. Multifactor theories apparently have added inconsequential factors to a basic theory that appears to be empirically inadequate. But, regardless of their shortcomings, multifactor theories have helped to identify many conditioning variables that must be taken into account in developing a valid theory of leadership in work: position in the hierarchy, degree of professionalism on the staff, the personality constellations within work groups, and the nature of the work performed (for example, policy formulation or implementation).

Situational theorists have been keenly aware of conditioning variables that influence leadership styles. F. E. Fiedler [6] has developed the most all-embracing situational theory of leadership. He has identified three situational characteristics that shape the type of leadership pattern basic to effective group performance: the positional power of the leader, the degree of structure in group tasks, and the satisfying character of leader-member relations. He converted each of those dimensions into a dichotomy, creating eight combinations of situations. He then discussed each situation in terms of its advantages for the leader. The most favorable situation includes good relations between the leader and the members of his group, structured tasks, and sufficient positional power to permit the leader to do his job. The leader's job is expected to be most difficult when the opposite conditions prevail. Fiedler has also suggested that group performance may be highest in these extreme groups when leaders are more distant from members. Less social distance is required of leaders in intermediate situations.

Despite its sophistication this formulation has serious weaknesses. First, one of the independent variables— the satisfying character of leader-member relationships—seems quite similar to the dependent variable leadership distance. Second,

<hr/>

[6] F. E. Fiedler, *A Theory of Leadership Effectiveness* (New York: McGraw-Hill, 1967).

it is difficult to know just what Fiedler's leadership-distance scale really measures. Each respondent is asked to think of the person whom he least prefers to work with and then to describe him in a series of choices between paired and opposing terms. Workers receiving low scores are classified as cold, aloof, and distant, but the validating evidence that Fiedler presents does not support this classification; in fact, it does not appear to support any kind of classification. It seems just as likely that so-called "distant leaders" simply have greater ability to discriminate among people. Third, using the NASA-2 data, Butterfield[7] found that two of Fiedler's dimensions—structure of tasks and leader-member relations—were independently related to effectiveness of the work group, so that these two dimensions may explain all the results obtained by Fiedler.

All these findings suggest that the social sciences are still a long way from developing a pragmatic theory of leadership applicable to a broad range of work situations. It is not our purpose in this chapter to develop such a theory, rather we shall attempt to move a step or two in that direction by identifying significant components of such a theory. Our strategy centers on two questions raised by the studies reported earlier. First, how important is leadership in the achievement of effectiveness? In Chapter 6 Butterfield found repeatedly that none of the multifactor theories that he studied predicted the effectiveness of the branches in the Office of Administration of the National Aeronautics and Space Administration. He speculated that no type of leadership was necessary to achieve effectiveness at the branch level. Perhaps in some situations little or no leadership is required in order for workers to be effective. This possibility must be checked because it contradicts that bedrock assumption of all leadership theories that some form of leadership is essential for effective performance. Second, are there certain organizational characteristics that intervene meaningfully in the relationships between leadership activities and organizational effectiveness? The research reviewed in this book emphatically indicates that there are. What are they? How can they be incorporated into a general theory of leadership?

[7] Butterfield, An Integrative Approach to the Study of Leadership Effectiveness in Organizations (Doctoral diss., The University of Michigan, 1968).

THE IMPORTANCE OF LEADERSHIP
IN ORGANIZATIONAL EFFECTIVENESS

One way to test the contribution of leadership to organizational effectiveness is to examine the correlations between measures of supervisors' effectiveness and the index of effectiveness. Such correlations for three Federal agencies are shown in Table 7-2. The amount of variance explained ranges from 9 to 21 percent, which means that in the average division at NASA supervision contributed about one-fifth of the input for effective performance. In the H.E.W. office studied supervision contributed only 10 percent.

TABLE 7-2 Correlations Between Perceived Effectiveness of Supervisors and Division Effectiveness

SITE	CORRELATIONS	NUMBER OF CASES
NASA-1	.46*	421
NASA-2	.44	409
Alpha Agency	.37	405
H.E.W.	.30	318

*All correlations are statistically significant beyond the .01 level.

But these correlations are only average figures for all divisions in each study. A more accurate measure of the contribution of supervision to effective functioning can be obtained from the intradivisional correlations. Accordingly, the eight divisions in the NASA-1 study that were large enough ($n = 20$ or higher) to produce stable correlations were selected for analysis. Correlations between supervisory and division effectiveness were obtained for each of the eight divisions. The range was between $r = .04$ and $r = .61$. Depending upon the division, the efforts of supervisors explained 0-36 percent of the variance in the effectiveness measure. Apparently the actions of leaders do make considerable difference in performance in some situations and little or none in others.

Although these tests are useful, they lack precision. We confronted the issue with considerably greater directness at H.E.W. by asking the following question of all respondents:

Some people say that what their supervisor does or does not do really has very little effect on the work that is done by those under him. Do you agree or disagree with this statement?

One of every five respondents thought that his supervisors really had "very little effect" on the work that was done. But, when the responses were examined by G.S. level, an interesting pattern emerged. One-third of the respondents at G.S. levels 1-7, fewer than one-tenth of those at G.S. levels 8-11, levels and none of those at G.S. level 12 or higher agreed with this statement. At the lower G.S. levels the value of supervision was least apparent. When these people were asked what factors did have important effects on the work done, they usually mentioned various aspects of the work process: the stage at which the work arrived, whether or not it arrived on time, the clarity of the job request, and whether or not equipment was working properly. These people were engaged in highly structured, repetitive batch production, and their productivity depended primarily upon effective coordination rather than upon their supervisors. When these respondents were asked how a supervisor could help them to do their work, two-thirds of them mentioned technical skills ("technical competence," "knows our jobs," "he can help us with our technical problems" and so on.) Administrative skills were also mentioned by almost two-thirds of the respondents, but their emphasis was mostly on techniques of administration, rather than on the quality of decisions. Fairness, skill in communicating, and willingness to treat everyone equally were most commonly mentioned. The only purely administrative activity that was mentioned frequently was "getting the work in here on time."

Among respondents at G.S. 12 or higher levels no one discounted the importance of supervision. But, *in addition* to the skills mentioned by respondents at lower G.S. level, this group mentioned many task- and support-oriented skills. These findings suggest that the importance of supervision in achieving effectiveness can be overemphasized. It appears to vary with certain organizational characteristics (like G.S. level). Furthermore, the specific supervisory activities relevant to effectiveness appear to vary with G.S. level and type of work. We expect that G.S. level is an indicator variable imperfectly associated with other characteristics of organization to determine which supervisory behaviors contribute to effective performance. The identification of some of these other characteristics is our task in the section which follows.

ORGANIZATIONAL CHARACTERISTICS
AND EFFECTIVE LEADERSHIP

As we suggested in Chapter 1, all leaders operate in organizations that are to some extent open systems; that is, they are permeable to their environments in varying degrees. The most fluid situation imaginable is an organization that is frequently affected by relevant environmental stimuli handled solely by formation of negotiated orders. If few examples of such situations come readily to mind, it is because members of organizations usually try to gain some control over environmental inputs (to reduce the openness of the organization) and to institutionalize some of the negotiated responses to certain stimuli. Leaders usually take a major share of the responsibility for reducing the openness of the organization. They can achieve some closure by regulating their environments; especially the physical environment can be manipulated so that it presents fewer problems. The range of products demanded by outsiders can be narrowed by shaping their tastes. Leaders can systematize the internal environment by solving problems, creating new routines, and adding new systems. They are thus involved in an input-output system in which their outputs include structuring tasks and relationships and perhaps some closure of the system. The inputs are new and relevant stimuli, or problems, whether internal or external.

But what are the implications for the leadership role if the rate of input exceeds the rate at which the leader creates output (structures)? We are describing an open-system leader whose continued involvement in organizational problem-solving contributes greatly to the effectiveness of his organization, and what happens when the leader creates and implements solutions more rapidly than new problems occur? The activities of all leaders are additive: As they solve problems and create new procedures, they reduce the necessity for their own involvement in the newly regulated activities. But in the gradually closing organization in which leadership output exceeds situational input this additive character takes on new significance. Each increment of solution leads to some diminution of the activities that the leader must perform, and his participation becomes less and less essential to the effectiveness of the organization.

In hierarchical organizations any or all parts of the hierarchy can be involved in reducing openness and systematizing the activities of any operating unit. A personnel office can be given the responsibility for recruiting new personnel; the department supervisors must then take the people assigned to them. The systems and time-and-motion engineers can structure work processes and specify the tasks involved in them, minimizing the number of internal adaptive problems. They can also structure inputs from other units.

The supervisor of the unit contributes to these activities by his own problem solving. But, as he and others continue this process, they contribute less and less to the effectiveness of the unit. The supervisor is reduced to bookkeeping: logging performance data, checking time cards, and scheduling vacations. He also performs some interface activities: reporting equipment breakdowns and input-output problems. Sometimes he is responsible for a human-relations program, for relations with shop stewards, or for keeping management informed of potential or actual labor problems. His most important qualification for effective performance is experience; he should know a lot about the jobs under his direction, the machinery used, and how emergencies have been handled in the past. His role is thus greatly reduced or, more accurately, dispersed among other men, machines, and rules, which suggests the following hypothesis: *As the outputs of organizational closure and structuring of processes increasingly exceed situational inputs, the number and range of supervisory behaviors related to effectiveness decrease.* Conversely, the more open the organization is and the less frequently past routines are applicable to current problems, the greater the number and range of leadership behaviors related to effectiveness. These conditions exist in many work situations: some research projects, program management, putting out fires, stopping riots, and so on. In such situations the leader can do much to help in the adaptive phases because usually he has experience, control of resources, access to specialists, and often intelligence at least as great as that of his subordinates.

Using system closure and routinization may help us to neutralize the inadequacies of hierarchical position (G.S. level in our case) as a conditioning variable. It may help us to explain

why the styles of effective management in high-level administration and in many forms of laboratory research are so
similar, though the hierarchical positions of such groups can
be considerably different. Both are usually relatively open
systems with long adaptive phases built into their work.

There are four basic forms of output that can increase
the closure of the organization and the routinization of its
processes: structuring inputs and input processes, structuring
outputs and output processes, structuring tasks, and structuring relationships among tasks (provided that the tasks are interdependent). In the next two sections of this chapter we shall
consider the last two forms of output. Our specific hypotheses
will be that *the number and range of leadership behaviors
correlated with the effectiveness of a work group are reduced
as the degree and prevalence of task structuring increases,*[8]
*the interdependence of tasks decreases, and the degree and
prevalence of structuring of relationships among interdependent
tasks increases.* We expect such correlations to exist in all situations but to be most apparent and to have their greatest impact
in organizations in which outputs of structuring exceeds inputs
of problems.

The Structuring of Tasks and Effective Leadership

Tasks are structured by means of two mechanisms: the
application of technology to the task and the development of
clusters of rather detailed norms governing the task. Although
these mechanisms appear different, in one respect they are actually isomorphic. The process of designing machinery involves
embedding norms in things, replacing human systems with
machine systems. Machines are embodiments of culture. When
they set the rhythm and pace of activities, then the supervisor
loses some aspects of his role, and the machine itself becomes
something of a supervisor.

The leadership function is also diffused by means of
formal or informal norms created to govern the techniques
and timing of work. Many such norms are developed inform-

---

[8] E. H. Burack, "Technology and Supervisory Functions: A Preliminary
View," *Human Organization* 26 (1967): 256-264; Burack, "Industrial Manage-
ment in Advanced Production Systems: Some Theoretical Concepts and Pre-
liminary Findings," *Administrative Science Quarterly* 12 (1967): 479-500; and
W. R. Rosengren, "Structure, Policy, and Style: Strategies of Organizational
Control," *Administrative Science Quarterly* 12 (1967): 140-164.

ally over time. They constitute part of the lore that the experienced worker brings to his job. In a work group with a high proportion of experienced and sufficiently motivated workers the contribution of the leader to effective performance should be correspondingly reduced.

Another characteristic of task structuring also affects the role of the supervisor. Structured task systems, particularly mass-production and automated systems, permit and even require short error-feedback loops. We say "permit" because structured tasks are usually sequences of very simple activities; because of this simplicity the worker can usually recognize and error and correct it himself. Or he can scan error-indicator panels to correct or stop the process himself. If he were to delay his response in order to ask the advice of his supervisor, valuable time would be lost; during that time the machinery would continue to produce defective products. For these reasons task structure can reduce the role of the supervisor as a problem solver.

This line of reasoning helps to explain J. Woodward's finding that mass-production systems permitted a broader range of supervisory control than did either batch or continuous-process systems.[9] Woodward actually found that many continuous-process tasks, for example, maintenance and repair tasks, involved batch or unique-product production. Task structure in batch production varied from sequences of structured tasks to sequences of tasks no two of which were alike and that therefore could not be structured profitably. Greater supervisory involvement was required to provide normative control in the latter instance. Similarly, in our NASA data we found that the degree of task structure had a small but revealing relationship with subordinates' estimates of their supervisors' authority ($r = -.24$, $n = 247$, $p < .01$); the greater the task structure, the more likely the supervisor was to be perceived as having little authority. Task structuring is a control system that competes with or supplants supervisors in some areas, perhaps even suggesting that supervisors are dispensable.

To test the effects of task structure on effective supervisory behavior in the NASA-1 data, we used the measure of

[9] J. Woodward, *Industrial Organization: Theory and Practice* (New York: Oxford University Press, 1965), pp. 60-63.

task structure described in Chapter 3 as a control on correlations between measures of supervisory behavior and division effectiveness. It should be recalled that this measure was an average score for all tasks in a division or branch and not a score for an individual task. The frequency distribution of task-structure scores was divided into three parts to obtain categories of high, medium, and low task structure.[10] The correlations between division effectiveness and supervisory behavior were obtained *within* each category of task structure (see Table 7-3).

When task structure was medium or low, virtually every measure of supervisory behavior was highly related to the index of division effectiveness. These findings can be summarized in the single finding that the perceived effectiveness of the supervisor was highly correlated ($r = .56$) with overall effectiveness. The same pattern emerged when the correlations between these measures of supervisory behavior and the indexes of productivity and adaptability were examined. The correlations of the supervisory measures with the measure of flexibility were only slightly lower than those with productivity and adaptability. The flexibility measure was highly correlated with the three measures of adequacy of conditions for negotiating orders when task structure was low. This finding confirms our earlier finding that in emergencies informal horizontal interaction and problem solving were valuable aids to leaders coping with emergencies.

When task structure was high, an almost opposite pattern occured. Few measures of supervisory behavior accounted for much variance in the effectiveness index. Technical skills

[10] The frequency distribution of task-structure scores and the categories derived from it are shown in this table.

SCORE INTERVALS	FREQUENCY	CATEGORIES OF TASK STRUCTURE
3.16-3.55	10	low
3.56-3.95	97	
3.96-4.35	19	
4.36-4.75	30	
4.76-5.15	21	medium
5.16-5.55	1	
5.56-5.95	27	
5.96-6.35	7	high
6.36-6.75	43	

TABLE 7-3 *Relationships Between Measures of Division Effectiveness and Supervisory Behaviors for Different Degrees of Task Structure, NASA-1*

SUPERVISORY BEHAVIOR	TASK STRUCTURE		
	HIGH	MEDIUM	LOW
Instrumental Skills			
Good technical skills	.36*	.32	.59
Knowledge of the jobs in respondents' areas	.27	.24	.30
Good administrative skills	.15	.49	.60
Helpful to employees when necessary	.33	.39	.46
Frequently causes loss of time through poor planning	−.37	−.61	−.56
Good human-relations skills	.06	.46	.45
Willingness to stand up for employees with his own supervisor	.26	.48	.53
Interpersonal Skills			
Belittling of employees	−.10	−.40	−.24
Frequent cause of annoyance	−.18	−.48	−.40
Openness of Interaction on Work Problems			
Openness to employee influence in decisions	−.07	.15	.49
Receptivity to employees' ideas about work problems	.27	.33	.43
Willingness to discuss work problems with employees	.14	.23	.25
Use of group or man-to-man techniques	.05	−.27	−.01
Authority			
Adequate authority for supervisory responsibilities	.05	.58	.28
Overall Effectiveness	.46	.54	.56
N	50	97	107
Significance at .05 level	.28	.20	.19
Significance at .01 level	.37	.26	.25

*Pearson product-moment correlations.

and providing assistance when necessary were the variables most strongly related to effectiveness. One finding is somewhat deceptive: the absence of correlation between division effectiveness and human-relations skills of the supervisor. Actually the latter variable was related to the measures of productivity and adaptability but not to that of flexibility (r = .32, .27, −.07 respectively). Supervisory mistakes because of poor planning were about as important to the effectiveness of work groups as were any positive supervisory efforts. Despite the diminished importance of supervision in high struc-

tured situations, the correlation between the overall effectiveness of the supervisor and that of his division was quite high
(r = .46), not much lower than that for situations in which
task structure was low (r = .56). This finding suggests that
there are other, unmeasured supervisory activities related to
the effectiveness of such work groups. We expect that these
activities include setting work standards and encouraging extra
effort, meeting workers' job needs, and establishing a reputation for fairness. No direct measures of these attributes were
included in the NASA-1 study, with the minor exception of a
measure of the supervisor's competence and fairness, which
was significantly correlated with division effectiveness (r =
.40) when task structure was low. But it is impossible to know
how much the element of fairness contributed to the correlation.

A test of the task-structure hypothesis was included in
the Byberry-2 study. Respondents were asked:

About how much of your work would you say is fairly
routine?

_____(1) Almost all of my work is fairly routine
_____(2) More routine than not
_____(3) About half of my work is routine; about half
            is not routine
_____(4) Most of it is not routine
_____(5) Almost all of it is not routine

The first two responses were combined to form the high task-
structure category and the last two to form the low task-structure category. Table 7-4 gives the Byberry-2 data parallel to the
NASA-1 data in Table 7-3.

The pattern of findings in NASA-1 was generally repeated
in the Byberry-2 data. The more routine the respondent's work
was, the less likely he was to associate the effectiveness of his
unit with certain types of supervisory behavior. This pattern
was repeated when the measures of productivity, adaptability,
and flexibility were substituted for overall effectiveness in the
correlations. Unfortunately, no measures of the supervisor's
technical skills were included in the Byberry-2 study. It would
have been interesting to see whether or not they were highly
correlated with unit effectiveness for highly structured tasks,
as they were in NASA-1.

TABLE 7-4 *Relationships Between Measures of Unit Effectiveness and Supervisory Behaviors for Different Degrees of Task Structure, Byberry-2*

SUPERVISORY BEHAVIOR	TASK STRUCTURE		
	HIGH	MEDIUM	LOW
Awareness of important problems	.21*	.40	.17
Effectiveness in solving problems	.09	.44	.42
Influence with own supervisors	.13	.25	−.07
Use of different points of view to make decisions in work group	.15	.43	.52
Belittling of employees	−.18	−.19	−.51
N	57	69	49
Significance at .05 level	.26	.24	.28
Significance at .01 level	.34	.31	.37

*Pearson product-moment correlations.

Despite certain inadequacies in the measures of task structure used here, the task-structure hypothesis did receive considerable support. When task structuring was high the number and range of supervisory behaviors related to effectiveness decreased. Technical skills appeared most valuable. Conversely, when task structure was low practically every supervisory behavior measured was related to unit effectiveness.

Task Interdependence, Structuring, and Effective Leadership

The hypothesis to be discussed in this section is that *the number and range of leadership behaviors related to the effectiveness of a work group decrease as the interdependence of tasks decreases and as the degree and prevalence of structuring of the relationships between interdependent tasks increase.* The number and range of leadership behaviors related to work-group effectiveness increase when the opposite conditions prevail and when interdependent tasks have not been routinized through formal coordination, or structuring.

Unfortunately, our attempts to test this hypothesis directly failed because in the setting available to us there was virtually no variation in the responses to a question about interdependence of tasks. Virtually all tasks were reported to be highly interdependent. Therefore a secondary analysis of NASA-1 data was undertaken in hopes of finding some indication of the potential usefulness of these hypotheses.

Let us assume that in divisions in which there was no relationship between measures of formal coordination of tasks and division effectiveness there was also little task interdependence. If the tasks were independent, we would expect no relationship between these two variables. The difficulty with this assumption is that there might also be no relationship between these variables when tasks were interdependent but had never been coordinated at all. In such an instance we would, however, expect the effectiveness of the division to be quite low. If in any given division there was no relationship between measures of formal coordination and division effectiveness and if division effectiveness was fairly high, we assume that task interdependence was low. The data from NASA-1 are arrayed according to this proposed test in Table 7-5.

The data from only eight of the twelve divisions were used because the other four seemed too small to produce stable correlation coefficients. Divisions D and J produced very low relationships between overall effectiveness and a measure of intertask coordination ("How well are the different jobs and work activities in your division geared together in the direction of meeting the objectives of the division?"). Fortunately, both had relatively high effectiveness scores, the highest among the divisions shown in Table 7-5. Our assumption of relative intertask independence was supported by our personal observations in these divisions. Division D was staffed by highly trained professionals who worked separately with outside clients to whom their division director assigned them. There was almost no need for them to share information about clients with one another. In Division J the work process began when clients from other parts of NASA called this division to request particular services. The secretary transferred each request to the appropriate supervisor, who assigned a specialist to take the needed action. These activities seldom involved joint action by two or more members of the division. Although the professional members of this division were less highly trained formally than were those in D, almost all had had long experience in their jobs and needed little help from others.

Table 7-5 shows that very little that the supervisors in those two divisions did facilitated effective performance. The exceptions were their uses of administrative skills and their ability to solve important problems. The supervisors were important in assigning clients or problems to specialists, in seeing that reasonable deadlines were met, and in helping special-

TABLE 7-5 Relationships Between Overall Division Effectiveness and Supervisory Behaviors, Controlled for Division, NASA-1

VARIABLES	DIVISION CODE							
	D	J	F	E	K	G	H	L
Intertask coordination †	.15*	.18	.35	.39	.41	.56	.56	.73
Supervisory behavior †								
Good technical skills	−.03	.09	.22	.27	.32	.26	.37	.56
Good administrative skills	.38	.40	.04	.27	.56	.21	.29	.53
Good human-relations skills	.13	.23	−.09	.41	.40	.62	.56	.66
Listens to workers' ideas about problems	.11	.13	−.20	−.10	.14	.49	.14	.28
Costs valuable work time through poor planning	−.09	.02	.09	−.56	−.46	−.49	−.43	−.44
Solves important problems well	.33	.37	.25	.41	.21	.13	.29	.53
Belittles employees	.08	.05	−.10	.04	−.16	.05	−.28	−.47
Has confidence in respondent	.13	.39	−.07	.32	−.02	.41	.45	.56
Uses different points of view in solving problems	.20	.30	−.01	.22	.38	.22	.31	.51
Is approachable	−.11	.08	.21	.19	.02	.35	.27	.47
General effectiveness	.08	.05	.28	.23	.41	.36	.36	.59
Overall division effectiveness, mean score	3.75	4.48	3.47	3.57	3.47	3.58	3.56	3.17
N	27	21	35	38	55	20	89	88

*Product-moment correlation between the overall effectiveness index and the variable shown at the left.
† This list does not exhaust the supervisory variables from the NASA-1 study; it was cut down for ease in presentation. No variable with high correlations in the first two columns was excluded, however.

ists to solve new problems as they arose. We suspect that a supervisor's skill as a trainer of specialists was also related to effectiveness, but no measure of that function was included in the questionnaire.

As the relationship between intertask coordination and division effectiveness increased, an increasing number of types of supervisory behavior were related to division effectiveness. In Divisions H and L virtually every kind of supervisory behavior listed was related to division effectiveness. In summary, this secondary analysis, despite its inadequacies, does suggest an important relationship between interdependence of tasks and various kinds of supervisory behavior.

PERSONAL CHARACTERISTICS AND PERFORMANCE AMONG LEADERS

In the preceding discussion we focused exclusively on situational factors that determined which kinds of supervisory behavior would facilitate effective performance. The role of personality in the functioning of work groups was not discussed. It seems likely that some personality factors have significant effects on work processes. For example, the supervisor's personality may influence which kinds of behavior he engages in and how well he performs, which may have effects on the overall performance of his work group. Although researchers have looked for a set of personality characteristics associated with leadership, or successful leadership, their efforts have yielded few consistent findings.[11] Yet it seems that certain mental traits or states ought to be associated with effective performance. Modern views of mental health are focused on how effectively a person can function in his roles.[12] The clear implication is that the presence of certain mental conditions are associated with dysfunctional role performance. Might

[11]There are several summaries of these findings. See, for example, R. M. Stogdill, "Personal Factors Associated with Leadership," *Journal of Psychology* 25 (1948): 35-71; C. A. Gibb, "Leadership," in *Handbook of Social Psychology*, II (Reading, Mass.: Addison-Wesley, 1954), pp. 877-920; R. D. Mann, "A Review of the Relationships between Personality and Performance in Small Groups," *Psychological Bulletin* 56 (1959): 141-170; B. A. Bass, *Leadership, Psychology, and Organizational Behavior* (New York: Harper & Row, 1960); and S. M. Sales, "Supervisory Style and Productivity: Review and Theory," *Personnel Psychology* 19 (1966): 175-286.

[12]Marie Jahoda, *Current Concepts of Positive Mental Health* (New York: Basic Books, 1958); and Leo Srole *et al.*, *Mental Health in the Metropolis: the Midtown Manhattan Study* (New York: McGraw-Hill, 1962).

not the presence of certain mental conditions then cause the supervisor to perform poorly in his job? The answer must be affirmative. In this short section we shall explore one small but provocative aspect of this question: behavioral correlates of the supervisor's level of anxiety.

The list of mental states and traits that might cause poor performance is quite long. Extreme and prolonged depression or loss of self-esteem can immobilize a supervisor, reduce his confidence in his own judgment, and increase his irritability and hostility toward others. Lack of ego strength can make him either impulsive or rigid in his demands for conformity. To test the general proposition that some mental characteristics of leaders influence their performance, we shall examine the relationship between anxiety and the performance of leadership functions. Anxiety has been selected because clinical psychologists and psychiatrists generally agree that the level of anxiety is one of the better indicators of mental health. Cattell and Scheier have distinguished two types of anxiety: characterological and situational.[13] The former is an aspect of personality predisposing the person to respond to certain stimuli as if they were threatening even when by objective standards they are not. His perceptions tend to be extremely subjective and irrational. Situational anxiety, on the other hand, is a realistic response to a genuine threat. Whereas situational anxiety fluctuates according to the situation, characterological anxiety remains fairly steady over time.

The Cattell Anxiety Test includes forty closed-end items that measure both kinds of anxiety.[14] It was administered to the twelve division directors and thirty branch managers in our NASA study. The overall anxiety scores (Sten scores) were computed according to Cattell's procedures. These data were then correlated with the mean responses of their subordinates to our effectiveness and supervisory items. As expected, no significant relationship between division or branch effectiveness scores and the levels of leaders' anxiety existed.

As we have already seen, in many situations leaders,

[13] R. B. Cattell and I. H. Scheier, *The Meaning and Measurement of Neuroticism and Anxiety* (New York: Ronald Press, 1961).
[14] For a description of this test, see Cattell and Scheier, *Handbook for the IPAT Anxiety Scale Questionnaire (Self Analysis Form)* (Champaign, Ill.: Institute for Personality and Ability Testing, 1963).

whether "good" or "bad," have only very limited effects on the functioning of their units. In other situations it is possible that the competence of the workers, the level of coordination among them, their ability to negotiate orders, and so on can cancel out some of the ill effects of dysfunctional leadership.

The level of the leader's anxiety is highly related to his role performance, however. Table 7-6 shows this relationship. The greater the anxiety of the leader, the less likely his subordinates were to report that he was effective. The source of this relationship is clear from the responses to other items: Anxious leaders received low evaluations on instrumental skills, interpersonal skills, and willingness to discuss work problems with their subordinates. They were sensitive to the power aspect in human relations, resisting the attempts of their subordinates to influence them, unwilling to go to bat for them at the next level up in the organization, and failing to represent the work group well at higher levels. The more anxious the leader, the more likely he was to supervise closely and to make major decisions himself. Such leaders had very little confidence and trust in their subordinates, and the latter were frequently annoyed with them.

Our data strongly suggest that how a leader performs his role is very much a function of his personality, particularly of his mental health. Perhaps a competent leader who is willing to take some risks, remains autonomous, and deals with people in a secure and supportive way is a product of personality predispositions *plus* training and experience, rather than only the latter. This conclusion seems obvious, yet few leadership programs seem to take it into account. Can the anxious leader profit significantly from a training program? It seems unlikely; much more intensive and sophisticated therapies are indicated. Our data suggest that mental-health criteria should be seriously considered along with the usual criteria for promotion. We are not proposing misguided "scientism," a paper-and-pencil test determination of who will lead. Rather we believe, first, that study of mental health is likely to produce many useful insights; second, that exposure to human-relations and other training is unlikely to improve significantly the performance of leaders with high levels of characterological anxiety; third, that many studies relating leaders' performance and work-group effectiveness have concentrated too much on *what* leaders do and not enough on *why* they do it; and finally, that in work situations requiring both intensive and extensive leadership (when the various forms of structuring are minimal) the highly anxious leader is extremely dysfunctional.

TABLE 7-6 *Relationships Between Levels of Anxiety and Role Behavior of Supervisors,* NASA-1

SUPERVISORY BEHAVIOR	RANK-ORDER CORRELATIONS WITH ANXIETY
Willingness to go to bat for respondent with his superiors	−.70
Good technical skills	−.62
Annoying to respondent	.60
Confidence and trust in respondent	−.60
Responsiveness to respondent's influence	−.57
Overall effectiveness	−.56
Understanding of respondent's work problems	−.53
Use of different points of view	−.49
Object of respondent's confidence and trust	−.47
Centralization of decision-making on major problems	.45
Grasp of respondent's ideas on work problems	−.44
Cause of lost time through poor planning	.43
Representation of work group	−.42
Receptivity to discussion of work problems	−.41
Institutional leadership	−.40
Belittling respondent	.39
Close supervision	.37
Good administrative skills	−.36
Effective problem solving	−.36
Human-relations skills	−.31
Approachability	−.19
Influence with own superiors	−.18
High work standards	−.18
Encouragement of team effort	−.16
Adequate authority for his responsibilities	−.15
Encouragement of extra effort	−.12
Guidance to improving performance	−.03
N	42

$r_s = .29$, significant at .05 level
$r_s = .39$, significant at .01 level

CONCLUSIONS

In this and the preceding chapter we have examined various theories of leadership, varying in the factors considered relevant and in the importance attributed to situational characteristics. All these theories have been found wanting in one or another fundamental way. Factor theories are troublesome because they combine types of leadership behavior in conceptually neat but often empirically invalid ways. Certain activities in a category may be related to effective performance in a given situation, whereas other activities in the same category may not be related. Furthermore, such findings are of little use to the practicing manager who wants to know what *specific* behaviors he should use to improve performance in his situation.

A more appropriate strategy would be to develop more exhaustive lists of specific areas of supervisory behavior, including items like "solves problems well," "encourages on-the-job training," and so on. Our own lists in these two chapters have not been exhaustive. The list used in the NASA-1 study was an amended version of an older list from human-relations research. In subsequent studies shorter, more eclectic, lists were used because of our multiple objectives. Our findings suggest, however, that a more exhaustive inventory of supervisory behavior, coupled with measures of unit effectiveness and task and process structuring, will yield important findings. Table 7-7 summarizes our findings and expectations

TABLE 7-7 *Task Interdependence, Structure, and Leadership Behavior*

TASK INTERDEPENDENCE AND INTERTASK STRUCTURE	TASK STRUCTURE	APPROPRIATE SUPERVISORY BEHAVIOR
High, unstructured	High	Build coordinating links between tasks, solve problems, and create conditions for negotiating orders
	Low	Beside those listed for High Task Structure, virtually all technical, administrative, and human-relations skills
High, structured	High	Routine administrative activities and solution to major adaptive problems
	Low	Fairly broad range of technical and administrative skills facilitating individual's efforts and unified direction of the work group
Low, structure irrelevant	High	Few technical and administrative activities. Primarily maintaining unified direction
	Low	Fairly broad range of individually oriented technical and administrative skills facilitating efforts of individual workers

from the consideration of the two internal forms of structuring. This table incorporates some situational assumptions. The functions of leadership need not be concentrated in a single role. Leadership is frequently diffused among norms and machines, as well as men. The types of leadership behavior concentrated in a role are only part of the directive activities of a group. In the effective group role-based leadership is complementary to that provided by norms, machines, and activities by other people who are informally negotiating order. We have proposed several conditions that shape leadership behavior relevant to group performance. Most involve structuring of inputs, outputs, tasks, or intertask processes. The degree of interdependence of tasks has also been recognized as a factor. Our data show that, as task structure increases, the number and range of leadership activities associated with effective performance decline. When task structure is high, supervisors' technical skills appear to be the most relevant to effective functioning. Relevant leadership behavior seems to be shaped by the degree of independence of tasks; as tasks become more independent, the administrative and adaptive (problem-solving) activities of leaders increase in importance. Further research along the lines suggested should yield a clearer picture of the relationships between leadership behavior and effectiveness.

Finally, our data show that the level of the leader's anxiety is highly related to how he fulfills his role. The anxious leader seems immobile and exhibits poor interpersonal relationships. These findings suggest two areas of study: What other mental traits and states are significantly related to leadership behavior? In what ways do work groups respond to anxious leaders?

8
Summary
and
Conclusions

In recent years our notion of what an organization is has undergone considerable change. Earlier models usually assumed a closed system with precise boundaries, the role was the unit of analysis, and structure was defined as routine interaction among roles. This approach was often adequate for analysis of the internal workings of organizations, but its weaknesses were immediately apparent whenever it was used in attempts to explain changes in organizations. Such concepts as lack of consensus on values or norms and role conflict helped somewhat, but in the end the approach was limited by the empirical inadequacy of its assumptions about closure. Human systems are open to their environments and are involved in various exchanges with those environments. That these exchanges can usually be controlled to some extent indicates that the degree of openness of organizations is variable, which in turn suggests a method of incorporating closed-system concepts into an open-system model of organization. As organizations vary in their degree of openness, which concepts provide the greatest explanatory and predictive power? A partial answer is suggested by Table 8-1. In the relatively open organization the concepts of role and formal coordination are still useful, but they are less important in understanding the organization than are concepts of the individual, improvising or negotiating structure, general goals and values, and leadership. If this line of reasoning is correct, then a useful open-system theory must incorporate social-psychological assumptions, as well as sociological ones.

This approach to organizations provides a useful perspective for understanding the differences in orientation of those who favor decentralized authority structures and those who favor highly structured organizations with fairly centralized authority systems (scientific management). For example, Warren G. Bennis has suggested that the adaptive activities of organizations are becoming increasingly important in our rapidly changing society.[1] Accordingly, he has favored an individual, rather than a role, orientation, freedom to solve

TABLE 8-1

KEY CONCEPTS	RELATIVELY CLOSED ORGANIZATIONS	RELATIVELY OPEN ORGANIZATIONS
Units of analysis	Roles, tasks, or sub-group tasks	Individuals and personal characteristics more important than roles
Interunit structuring	Routine interaction, formal coordination (structure)	Informal negotiation of new and perhaps temporary routines becomes increasingly important (process)
Clarity of the normative environment	Formal norms regulating tasks and inter-task relationships	General goals and objectives become increasingly important
Leadership	A narrow range of activities related to effectiveness	A broad range of activities related to effectiveness

problems informally, and the importance of clear goals and objectives. On the other hand, those who favor scientific management usually place greater emphasis on productivity and consider structuring as a means of achieving efficient production.

The differences between these two orientations could be resolved if the energies of their proponents were directed toward isolating the criteria that determine whether any given organization will be most effective when relatively open or relatively closed. That is, how open or closed should a given organization be in order to maximize its effectiveness? In many divisions of the National Aeronautics and Space Administration the extent of task and interface structuring was positively related to effectiveness, yet in other divisions these variables

[1]Warren G. Bennis, *Changing Organizations* (New York: McGraw-Hill, 1968).

were not related at all. We did not take up this question in our research, but its answers have important practical applications. Some overzealous leaders undoubtedly overstructure tasks and interface relationships in their work units, whereas others do not do enough. What guidelines to the appropriate levels of structuring can research provide? Obviously the appropriate levels of structuring are functions of the degree of closure that the organization can maintain without significantly impairing adaptability and flexibility. At this point, however, our terms become fuzzy because the area is still relatively unexplored. It is necessary to find a research design that uses numerous similar units (like hospitals and post offices), computes the ratios of adaptability and flexibility to productivity in each unit, and relates these ratios to the independent variables discussed here.

We also believe that many insights can be obtained through development of the interface concept and the design of research to study the effects of different types of interfaces on organizational effectiveness, on interorganizational conflict and problem-solving, and on facets of mutual understanding among groups. The concept of interface was to some extent explained in Chapter 1, but no measures of it had been included in our questionnaires because they required considerable space in already overburdened instruments. Recently we included such measures in a study of the Social and Rehabilitation Service of the Department of Health, Education and Welfare, and the findings will be reported in future publications.

One final note about the properties of organizations used or developed in this study is necessary. Organizations are power systems in which the configurations can reflect varying degrees of centralization and integration. In actual configurations of power none of the government agencies studied here even vaguely resembled the classic "ideal bureaucracy," though some of their smaller units did. All the "bureaucracies" with which we had contact had fairly decentralized and unintegrated power configurations. They were also surprisingly open systems. The more we studied them, the more we came to believe that the differences between them and other organizations studied by social scientists, say communities, were differences of degree, rather than of kind, and that combining organizational and community models and research findings can produce a useful, general model for both types of setting.

The use of parallel measures of configurations of power, authority, and decision-making raises an interesting research question. What are the effects on the structure of decision-making—and other aspects of organization—of similarities and dissimilarities between the configurations of power and authority? When power was fairly decentralized and authority was fairly centralized—the common characteristics of the government agencies that we studied—many subgroups acted as veto groups, obstructing effective action, reducing adaptability, and lowering morale generally. A variety of influencing techniques, with emphasis on persuasion and the cultivation of personal relationships, was used; interunit committees were also very common. This aspect of organizational life deserves closer attention.

DEFINING AND MEASURING
ORGANIZATIONAL EFFECTIVENESS

Within the conceptual framework of organization described briefly here, organizational effectiveness became the main object of study. It was defined as the relative ability of the members of an organization to mobilize their centers of power to produce, adapt, and handle temporally unpredictable overloads of work. This definition was intended to be as free of goal orientation as possible and to focus on the effectiveness of actual work processes, rather than on whether or not those processes were the most appropriate for achieving certain goals. This approach has both its strengths and its weaknesses. It avoids the arbitrariness of selecting managerial goals or those found in corporate charters as frames of reference; goals that may be vague, not universally accepted, or simply mask the real objectives of the organization. On the other hand, without such a frame of reference it is quite possible according to our measures to say that an organization is effective, yet ought to be doing something else. Our approach probably could be improved by the inclusion of questions measuring the extent to which an organization successfully pursues various goals that we select.

The advantages and disadvantages of using subjective measures of effectiveness are discussed in detail in Appendix A. The evidence suggest that, with appropriate safeguards, workers' subjective judgments provide a fairly valid measure of effectiveness. The major safeguard required is an outside evaluation of the effectiveness of the units under study. This evaluation will reveal any disagreements between inside and outside evaluators over the criteria of effectiveness and leave to social scientists the responsibility for resolving them. A second safeguard of some value would be using the goal-achievement measures just described.

THE CORRELATES OF EFFECTIVENESS
Decision-Making Configurations

Generally no necessary relationship between the degree of centralization of decision-making and any measure of effectiveness was found. The one exception occurred in the highly centralized organization, in which effectiveness seemed lower either in some settings or in relation to different components of the measure of effectiveness. We explain this exception not by pointing to some intrinsic weakness of the centralized decision-making configuration but by noting the unique relationship between this configuration and values in our society. First, the centralized configuration is rarely considered legitimate in our culture, and we showed in Chapter 4 that, the greater the legitimacy attributed to the configuration of decision-making of a work group, the greater effectiveness its members attributed to it. Second, as power is frequently uninfluenced by cultural values in our society, the centralized decision-making configuration can be very unpleasant for those subject to it, for they are vulnerable to whims that can be irrational, capricious, or motivated by a desire for self-aggrandizement. In future studies with larger numbers of respondents the perceived presence or absence of cultural values in the decision-making processes will be studied for its relationships with effectiveness, morale, and so forth. Are centralized configurations with rational-trust leaders any less effective than less centralized configurations which are also characterized by rationality and trust? We are not particularly interested in building a case for centralization of decision-making; that is not the task of a social scientist. But in this study we have been interested in testing the defense built up for decentralized decision-making. That evidence has been found wanting.

Our data also showed that effectiveness was greater in organizations with multiple elites when these elites were functionally and normatively integrated. Such integration permitted organizations to achieve unity of direction in their activities. Adaptability was greater because there were regular channels through which orders about change could pass and because potential resisters to change found no sympathetic elite to protect them from compliance to the orders. Only in emergencies for which no plans existed was an integrated elite of no use. Flexibility in such situations seemed more likely in less structured organizations.

General Organizational Characteristics

Our research has documented the importance of using open- and closed-system characteristics as intervening variables in many hypotheses about organizations. One method is to use tasks and intertask structuring as measures of system closure. Task structure is a role-oriented concept that measures the extent to which necessity for improvisation has been removed from the task. A computer program is currently the ultimate form of task structuring. Intertask structuring is the extent to which improvisation in both form and content of interaction has been rendered unnecessary or undesirable. When task structure and intertask structure are high the organization is relatively closed. The natural history of most groups (like mobs or clubs) involves evolution from low levels of task and intertask structure to relatively higher levels. The development of organized responses to disasters for which no plans exist reflects a similar shift in structuring.

All three survival processes—productivity, adaptability, and flexibility—can be structured to varying degrees, and the degree affects the organizational characteristics associated with them. Production, for example, can be highly rationalized and mechanized with precise, detailed job descriptions and equally precise, detailed plans of coordination linking jobs. None of our research settings offered examples of highly structured survival processes: no assembly-line production, no PERT programmed research, no automatic responses to emergencies. But, though variability in structure was thus somewhat less, task structuring was still an important intervening variable in productivity and flexibility. It was less important in studying the correlates of adaptability because it was more a function of organizational integration and structuring is only one of many ways to integrate the centers of power in an organization. When task structuring was high productivity was maximal in settings characterized by adequate coordination, opportunities for negotiating orders, and workers competent to perform their tasks. The clarity of the normative environment contributed little to maximizing productivity in such situations, and the range of leadership skills required for effective operation was reduced to a few technical and interface activities. But when tasks were relatively unstructured productivity was at its greatest when all of the characteristics just mentioned were abundantly present. A broad range of leadership skills was related to productivity because the leader had to provide advice, guidance, and resources during the improvising phases of work. A clear normative environment also facilitated production by providing a set of potential guidelines for improvisational problem solving. Levels of skills, formal coordination, and conditions for negotiating orders were also highly related to less structured productivity.

No direct measures of the degree of task or intertask structure for emergencies were obtained, but we know that in the hospitals that we studied emergency responses were unplanned and unstructured. In the government agencies emergencies resembled normal conditions telescoped into shorter time periods, and the structuring used in normal production could therefore also be used to some extent in emergencies. In these agencies we found that essentially the same organizational characteristics related to moderately structured productivity were related to flexibility as well, a pattern quite different from that in the hospitals. No measures of organizational or cultural integration were related to flexibility. As Table 8-1 suggests, the concepts of person, process, and improvisation are more useful in open system situations than are role and structure. In keeping with this view, we found that personal and background characteristics like length of service, professional training, and previous experience with emergencies were associated with unstructured flexibility.

Length of service and professional training appeared to have negative effects on adaptability; the older professional, imbued with the traditional tenets of his profession, was often reluctant to accept newer ways of doing things. Otherwise adaptability was a function of the normative and functional integration of the organization. Leadership had an important role in adaptive processes. When leaders solved organizational problems promptly and well, they preserved the integrated characters of their organizations. The core function of effective management was adaptive, involving a willingness to recognize problems and to solve them, to reallocate resources if necessary, and to venture into uncharted areas entailing some risk. Leadership is not for the insecure and anxious person. Yet how often do we encounter the anxious manager who concentrates on routine production and prefers the status quo to the unknown consequences of change?

Organizational Needs and Individual Needs

In a recent article Bennis[2] wrote: "Nevertheless, organizations frequently do not know what is truly rewarding, especially for professionals and highly trained workers who will dominate the organizations of the future. With this class of employee, conventional policies and practices regarding incentives, never particularly sensitive, tend to be inapplicable." Bennis meant primarily economic rewards, but his observation also serves as a good general summary of one area of our findings on individual needs. It is clear that our respondents preferred rational and fair normative work environments and opportunities to use their skills jointly with hard-working people on challenging tasks. The desire to do challenging work is not surprising from the point of view of what social scientists have learned about the bases for the formation of self-esteem by individuals. The desire for a rational and fair normative environment is also easy to understand. Most human beings thrive under conditions of fairness and rationality. Children do not like caprice, irrationality, and unfairness in their parents and adults do not like these qualities in their supervisors. These qualities reduce the predictability of behavior and complicate the calculation of one's own future.

Yet the needs for rational environment and challenging work were the least likely to be met. Why did organizational leaders go to such lengths to provide for needs that are less valued and not related to effectiveness and ignore needs that are important, related to organizational effectiveness, and far less costly to satisfy? Bennis has suggested ignorance, and he is undoubtedly correct. But we suspect that there are also intrinsic organizational and cultural factors that make these

[2]Bennis, "Post-Bureaucratic Leadership," *Trans-action* 6 (July-August 1969): 44-51, 61.

particular needs difficult to satisfy, factors like communication processes, distance, improper staffing, and so forth. We must learn what these factors are and how much each contributes to organizational failure to satisfy needs related to effectiveness.

More generally, we have found that the effective organization is one in which both organizational and individual needs receive high priority. When the manager creates an effective work environment in which problems of communication and coordination can be solved promptly and well, in which normative clarity and rationality are maintained, in which conditions for negotiating orders are adequate, in which work is challenging, and so on, he is meeting both organizational and individual needs. Those who favor the syrupy form of human relations—being friendly, knowing each worker's name and how many children he has, distributing selectively a little bag of rewards—have done a great disservice to management by obscuring its real responsibilities and the real needs of workers.

Leadership

The development of leadership theory fits neatly into the classic categories of dialectic. In the thesis phase a proposition was advanced: Democratic supervision is related to high morale and productivity. An antithesis supported by research findings followed: There is no necessary relationship between democratic supervision and either morale or productivity. There emerged a new synthesis combining some elements of the thesis with some findings from the antithesis. Both task leadership and socioemotional leadership are required for high morale and productivity. But even this new synthesis fails to stand up to testing, and the dialectic continues. We have attempted to chart some of these steps in Chapters 6 and 7. D. Anthony Butterfield has shown that multifactor theories are no better at predicting division effectiveness than are two-factor theories and are of no use at all in predicting branch effectiveness. He has also shown that F. Fiedler's situational theory of leadership has only very limited utility in predicting division effectiveness.[3]

[3] D. A. Butterfield, "An Integrative Approach to the Study of Leadership Effectiveness in Organizations" (Doctoral diss., The University of Michigan, 1968).

We have proposed three steps as a beginning toward developing a more useful leadership theory. First, we would discard the assumption that leadership automatically makes a significant contribution to group effectiveness. Then we can ask under what conditions does or does not leadership contribute significantly to group effectiveness? Second, two such conditions are the degree of task structuring and the degree of structuring of interdependent tasks. The impact of these conditions was summarized in Table 7-7. When task and intertask structure was high, the range of significant leadership skills dwindled to a few technical, administrative, and interface skills. Leadership was diffused among machines, rules, and other people. But, when structuring was low, a very broad range of leadership skills was related to effectiveness. Clearly, the more open the organization, the more important a broad range of leadership skills is to the effectiveness of the organization. Third, it might be useful to deal less with categories of leadership skills and to focus more on specific leadership activities. Such categories as democratic leadership, task leadership, and facilitation of interaction can be very misleading because specific activities can easily be placed in several different categories. Furthermore, any given activity can be interpreted variously, depending upon the situation in which it occurs. These reasons are all theoretical, but there is also one very important practical reason for concentrating on specific activities: The leader who tries to apply social science findings in practice can do so more readily and more effectively if he can adopt specific practices, rather than categories of practices.

ONE OR TWO CONCLUSIONS

Any number of conclusions and recommendations for further research are scattered through the preceding chapters as well as through this summary. They do not have to be repeated here, instead we should like to offer two fresh conclusions.

First, those practicing managers who may have read this book because of the implied promise in its title, hoping to find clear information that a single organizational framework or leadership style is related to effectiveness, have been disappointed. Single prescriptions for effectiveness are like mirages: desirable but distant, receding, unreal. Our research shows that various styles of leadership and organizational structure can be effective. It is necessary to rely on the conditioning factors that have been discussed here to determine the appropriate techniques and structures to use. Selection of the appropriate decision-making structure is influenced by the legitimacy of the various alternative structures, the proportion of professionals on the staff, whether or not an emergency exists, the degree of improvisation involved in the work, and so forth. Similarly, the degree of task and intertask structure affects how other organizational characteristics are related to effectiveness. There are thus usually several ways of organizing and leading that will yield about the same levels of effectiveness.

There is one set of findings that cannot be treated quite so flexibly, however: the findings on organization and individual needs. Managers must design and maintain organizations in which people can work. They must also develop people. It is pointless to stockpile talent and then not to use it; high turnover rates, alienation, and poor performance can be the only consequences of such practices. The development of people entails provision of meaningful work and work situations and opportunities to test abilities.

Second, among the many schools of thought in the social sciences there are at least two that seem to have been at odds. One school embraces the values and perspectives of "management" and does management-oriented research. The second questions the values of the first, claiming that such a focus ignores crucial issues like the organization of the national economy itself (for example, control by owners versus control by workers). Behind such claims is a fundamental identification with the worker and a desire that his work be psychologically meaningful and rewarding to him. The research reported here shows that these two views can be combined. We began with a question from the management orientation: What are the characteristics of effective organizations? But we quickly found that the answers involve the nature of the work itself. In any organization the personal needs that workers most want fulfilled are the very needs whose fulfillment facilitate organizational effectiveness.

Appendixes

A
The Validity
of the
Effectiveness Measures

In their study of ten community general hospitals in Michigan Basil S. Georgopoulos and Floyd C. Mann designed and attempted to validate subjective measures of the quality of patient care, which is a criterion similar to our quality of production. The researchers reasoned that so-called "hard criteria" measures, like comparative infant-mortality rates, are difficult to obtain and individually measure at best only limited facets of the quality of patient care.[1] Their strategy was to obtain clinical judgments from professionals—physicians and nurses— and to compare them with various hard-criteria measures. The use of clinical judgments was based on the assumption that qualified judges like physicians can make valid evaluations of the quality of patient care given in hospitals with which they are affiliated because they use rational professional criteria. It was assumed that most physicians would judge the medical care in a hospital by such standards as promptness of admissions procedures, accuracy and rapidity of laboratory and radiological examinations, competence of nursing staff, and administration of prescribed therapies at prescribed times in prescribed ways. To be sure, some physicians would not use rational professional criteria, but it was hoped that they would be in a minority and that their judgments would cancel one another out.

There was evidence from earlier studies to suggest that this line of reasoning had considerable merit.[2] A Likert-scale

[1]Basil S. Georgopoulos and Floyd C. Mann, *The Community General Hospital* (New York: Macmillan, 1962), pp. 198-264.
[2]See Robert L. Kahn and Daniel Katz, "Leadership Practices in Relationship to Productivity and Morale," in *Group Dynamics: Research and Theory*, ed. D. Cartwright and A. Zander (New York: Harper & Row, 1953), pp. 612-

item designed to measure the quality of medical care was therefore administered to the physicians affiliated with each of the ten hospitals in the study. The mean scores for all physicians in each hospital were calculated and then ranked and correlated with other data. This measure was found to be significantly related to the evaluations of these hospitals by a panel of outside physicians whose work brought them into contact with most of the hospitals. It tended to be related to the infant-mortality rate (excluding stillbirths) r_s = .47. The latter measure was significantly related (r = $-.66$) to evaluation of the quality of nursing care by the doctors and nurses in each hospital. These and the other data offered are by no means a conclusive demonstration of the validity of subjective measures of effectiveness. No one is more aware of this inadequacy than are the researchers themselves, who are currently engaged in an ambitious effort to test the validity of their measures against a hard-criteria index prepared by a panel of doctors. Although the final report has not been made at this writing, preliminary analyses of these comparisons for fifty-one hospitals have been quite encouraging.[3] It had been found in the earlier study that the judgments of hospital employees who were not physicians— nurses, laboratory technicians, and key administrative personnel—were significantly related to those of the physicians. This finding suggests that other groups in the hospital were capable of making evaluations by essentially the same criteria as those used by physicians.

NASA-1

Further tests of the validity of subjective measures of effectiveness were included in our study of the Office of Administration at the National Aeronautics and Space Administration. This office was composed of many divisions, twelve of which were large enough to yield sufficient data for analysis. The work of these divisions was only slightly interrelated, for the clients of most of them were located elsewhere in the organization. A questionnaire that included items designed to measure organizational effectiveness was administered to all

628; and Georgopoulos and Arnold S. Tannenbaum, "A Study of Organizational Effectiveness," *American Sociological Review*, 22 (October 1957): 534-540.

    [3] Personal communication from Georgopoulos.

full-time personnel who had worked in their respective divisions for more than six months. Four hundred thirty-eight completed questionnaires were obtained, a 90 percent response rate.

To learn whether or not any occupational categories had answered the questions differently from the others, we controlled the following categories—division directors and branch chiefs, other supervisors, nonsupervisory professionals, nonsupervisory nonprofessionals, and secretaries—and examined the responses of each to the effectiveness items. No statistically significant differences appeared in any of the occupational groups. The nonsupervisory professionals evaluated productivity in their divisions slightly less favorably than did other categories, but they gave slightly more favorable responses to the adaptability items than did the others. None of these differences came close to significance, even at the .10 level.

The product-moment correlations among these items in the NASA data were shown in Table 2-2. The individual items tended to be correlated more highly with other items in the same conceptual area (either productivity, adaptability, or flexibility) than with items from different areas. But few of these correlations were especially high; most were in the .30s and .40s. Each item appeared to be measuring a substantially different aspect of the concept of effectiveness. Similar tables for the other organizations studied are shown in Appendix C; they reveal essentially the same pattern as do the data from NASA.

A factor analysis of the effectiveness items and some systems items is shown in Table A-1. The first factor was clearly a productivity measure. The second factor combined measures of the input-output system and, to a lesser extend, of flexibility and symbolic adaptability. The third factor included the items measuring behavioral adaptability. A factor analysis of the effectiveness items in Georgopoulos and Mann's data produced comparable results. Three factors emerged: quality of patient care, behavioral adaptability, and flexibility. The measures of symbolic adaptability were not used in that study. These and other varimax rotations of the enumerated items from our other studies reveal that in general there was no problem of response set for most items. The major exception was the question about the extent to which people kept abreast of developments in technology and methods. This item was consistently loaded on more than one factor.

The overall effectiveness scores for the twelve divisions studied in NASA are shown in Table A-2. Two of the divisions were judged considerably more effective than were the others,

TABLE A-1 Factor Analysis* of Responses to Items by All Personnel, NASA-1

Division production				
Quantity	.79804	.05402	.09588	−.03856
Quality	.75238	.12298	.17448	.01142
Efficiency	.82382	.16201	.16505	−.04236
Availability of materials and informa-				
tion	−.10056	.63822	.14556	−.00311
Ease of distributing division products	.14221	.76775	−.01500	.08595
Ease of division recruitment	−.06139	.21895	.28136	.54311
Top-management control over routines	.25450	.57553	.10329	−.10171
Ease of deviating from top manage-				
ment's prescriptions	.04041	−.11519	−.17676	.84740
Division adaptation				
Anticipating problems	.39949	.45515	.34306	.04930
Keeping abreast of new methods	.42586	.51844	.28519	.12786
Rapidity of adjustment	.22286	.15695	.85238	−.00112
Prevalence of adjustment	.21444	.12790	.84808	.01018
Division flexibility	.44227	.46589	.13147	.13587

*Varimax Rotated Factor Matrix (Normalized Solution); factor contributions:
1   2.61434
2   2.16749
3   1.87145
4   1.07156
sum 7.72484

and two of them judged themselves considerably less effective than did the others. The rest were closely grouped between, where slight changes in scores would have significant effects on the ranking of the divisions. From our two and a half years of work in these twelve divisions we concluded that the dividing line between essentially functional and essentially dysfunctional divisions occurred somewhere in the neighborhood of a 3.75 mean score on the effectiveness index.

Hard-criteria measures of division effectiveness were impossible to obtain because of the diversity and complexity of the work of the twelve divisions. Instead we selected two other validating strategies. First, the top management of the Office of Administration ($N = 4$) was asked to evaluate the effectiveness of each division, using the same criteria that our division respondents had used. Second, division respondents were asked to evaluate the effectiveness of other divisions with

TABLE A-2 Division Mean Scores of Effectiveness, NASA-1

	DIVISION											
	A	B	C	D	E	F	G	H	I	J	K	L
Respondents' mean effectiveness scores for their own divisions	3.56	4.00	3.46	3.81	3.32	3.18	3.66	3.69	4.36	3.79	3.82	3.49
Rank-orders of mean scores	8	2	10	4	11	12	7	6	1	5	3	9

which they had fairly frequent contact. Each member of the top-management team was interviewed separately. He was given a pack of twelve cards, each with the name of a division on it; through a process of paired comparisons he ranked the divisions' effectiveness according to our criteria. Two of these respondents tended to agree in their rankings, but the other two did not agree with the first two or with each other. A composite rank ordering was constructed, and the results are shown in Table A-3.

The rank-order correlations—between self-ratings and top-management ratings = .72, between self-ratings and ratings by people in other divisions = .55 are statistically significant at the .01 and .05 levels respectively. The top management and people in other divisions rank orders correlate significantly, r_s = .77.

TABLE A-3 Rankings of the Divisions by Various Groups, NASA-1

DIVISION	SELF-RATINGS	TOP-MANAGEMENT RATINGS	RATINGS BY PEOPLE IN OTHER DIVISIONS
A	8	10	7
B	2	3	5
C	10	4.5	2
D	4	6	4
E	11	11	11
F	12	12	12
G	7	7	10
H	6	2	6
I	1	1	3
J	5	4.5	1
K	3	8	8
L	9	9	9

These correlations suggest considerable agreement on the relative effectiveness of the various divisions. Respondents showed a strong tendency to rate other divisions more favorably than they rated their own.

In order to understand the limitations of our measures, it is helpful to analyze the situations in which the greatest variation among rankings of the divisions assigned by the various raters occurred. Divisions C and H accounted for most such variation. Much of Division C's work was secret, and outside contact with it was quite limited. Outside evaluations of this division accurately reflected such contacts, as well as the reputation for competence of its director. But the people within the division did not share outsiders' views of the competence of their division director. On measures of effectiveness he was rated among the three lowest. More important, his actions were considered detrimental to the functioning of the division. The employees of this division also perceived that their mission was becoming less necessary to NASA and that the division was overstaffed. This recognition created a "make work" atmosphere in the division that the employees did not like. Their responses to the quantitative item in the productivity index were more than three standard deviations below the mean score for all twelve divisions.

Division H was a very large division, one of the few that interacted with all the others; it provides supplies and various services to them. It had extremely high established standards of service to others; those standards are maintained at the expense of high pressure and stress within the division. Consequently, outsiders evaluated it more favorably than its own members did.

NASA-2

One and a half years later in March 1967, a second questionnaire was administered in the same twelve divisions of NASA. A few months after the first questionnaire had been administered, the major findings had been discussed in detail with three-quarters of the personnel in the Office of Administration. Division directors and their branch chiefs had been given opportunities to use the data to identify problems and to solve them. A report on the efficacy of those activities will be made separately.

The effectiveness items and all the other key questions from the first instrument were included in the second; 432 completed questionnaires were obtained, a 92 percent response rate. The division effectiveness scores of the first round were correlated (r_s = .68) with the second-round scores. As a new

TABLE A-4 *Summary of Division Ranks on Effectiveness Measures, NASA-2*

DIVISIONS	SELF-RATINGS ON EFFECTIVENESS		COMPOSITE RANKINGS BY DIVISION DIRECTORS	COMPARATIVE EFFECTIVENESS*	FULFILLMENT OF MISSION**
	MEAN	RANK			
A	3.72	7	10	11	11
B	4.25	2	2	3	3
C	4.00	4	5.5	5	6.5
D	3.79	5	3	2	4
E	3.74	6	10	7	6.5
F	3.61	11	12	8	10
G	3.71	8	10	9	8
H	3.64	9	4	10	5
I	4.65	1	1	1	1
J	4.07	3	5.5	4	2
K	3.62	10	8	6	9
L	3.23	12	7	12	12
Ranking correlations†					
Self-ratings on effectiveness			.66	.80	.85
Composite rankings by division directors			-	.66	.77
Comparative effectiveness			-	-	.83

*Comparative effectiveness was measured by a single item: "Compared to other government groups you have worked in before coming to NASA (or NACA) how would you rate the effectiveness of *your present division?*"

**Fulfillment of mission was also measured by a single item: "Taking all things into consideration, how well do you feel your division does in fulfilling its mission or achieving its goals?" These two were summary items that followed immediately after the last effectiveness items. The index items, however, did not appear contiguously.

†All correlations were significant at the .05 level.

top-management team had just been installed, we did not ask for its evaluations of the divisions, for its members barely knew the names of the division directors, much less the functioning of the divisions. Instead we administered to the division directors the same paired comparisons that we had used with top management in the first round. The division directors did not have to rank divisions that they did not feel competent to rank. The results are shown in Table A-4.

Again, there is ample consistency among the ratings to warrant confidence in the effectiveness measures. Division H exhibited the same pattern that it had exhibited in the earlier study and for the same reasons. Division L was the other division for which significant differences between inside and outside evaluations appeared. During the one and a half years between the administrations of questionnaires existing organizational and personality problems had become increasingly severe, but their impact had not been felt by the other divisions at the time of NASA-2. (Since then the impact has spread, and the division has lost one of its major functions to other, more effective units.) Some units in Division E had successfully solved problems revealed in the data of NASA-1, but the rest of the division remained essentially unchanged.

So far two problems related to the validity of evaluations by outside judges have emerged: the visibility of the division's work and the time lag between improvements in internal operations and their external effects. On the other hand, the self-appraisals of the division members seem to have withstood the various tests of their validity. The study at Alpha Agency, however, did reveal a problem with self-appraisals of effectiveness.

Alpha Agency

The instruments used were again questionnaires that included many core items from the NASA instruments (occasionally modified to fit the jargon of Alpha Agency) and some new items designed to investigate some suggestive leads yielded by the NASA studies. In all, 423 completed questionnaires were obtained from the eligible population, a 96 percent response rate. In all *divisional* analyses of the data those from two units (fifty-one respondents) have been excluded. The first was the Personnel Division, which had only five respondents, an inadequate number for analysis. The second was the Office of the Administrator, which encompassed a potpourri of disparate functions defying logic. The management function of the Office of the Administrator was also excluded, in order to maintain the necessary parallels with the NASA data, in which the director's office was treated as a separate level, to which all units in the Office of Administration were responsible. In all other analyses these two groups have been included.

Alpha Agency was divided into fourteen units. In thirteen units the numbers of respondents ranged from thirteen to fifty-one; only four had fewer than twenty respondents.

Analyses of the responses to the effectiveness measures by different occupational categories revealed no appreciable differences, statistically or otherwise, among the categories. Furthermore, about one-third of the nonprofessional respondents were concentrated in a service division similar to Division

H in NASA. The rest, secretaries and clerical personnel at relatively high G.S. levels, were scattered thinly throughout the agency. Unit-effectiveness scores were therefore overwhelmingly those of professional people; the ranking of those scores is shown in Table A-5.

TABLE A-5 Comparisons of Divisions on Different Measures of Effectiveness, Alpha Agency

DIVISION CODE	EFFECTIVENESS INDEX		SUCCESS AT ACHIEVING OBJECTIVES	RATINGS BY PEOPLE IN OTHER UNITS
	MEAN	RANK*		
A	3.83	6	7	8
B	3.75	10	9.5	2
C	3.49	12	4	10
D	3.34	13	12	9
E	3.98	1	2	13
F	3.80	8	9.5	5
G	3.93	3	3	1
H	3.59	11	8	6
I	3.76	9	11	11
J	3.86	5	1	3
K	3.95	2	5	4
L	3.87	4	13	12
M	3.82	7	6	7

*The number 1 is assigned to the unit with the highest score (the most effective unit) and so on.

The single summary item, which is stated in goal terms (success at achieving objectives) was barely related to the effectiveness index at the .05 level: r_s = .48. Two divisions, C and L, accounted for almost all the unexplained variation. For Division C the variation partly reflects the frailties of using rank orders, rather than actual mean scores; the mean score on the index and the item were actually quite similar, 3.49 and 3.68 respectively. But the scores for all units were generally lower on the latter item (overall mean = 3.45) than they were on the index (X = 3.75), reflecting one of the most fundamental problems of Alpha Agency: a prevalent feeling among the members that the agency had excellent personnel organized to do a good job but receiving little direction from top management on objectives of their work. For example, the overall mean score of the Administrator's Office on setting goals and general work programs was 3.12 (somewhat unsuccessful). That on ability to provide general management was 3.04 (somewhat unsuccessful). But just at the time of our study top management had completed its own study of Division C and had defined its mission, with the concomitant requirement that it reshape its internal operations. Some of the disparity between measure can be attributed to this period of transition. But there was nothing in the situation to warrant questioning the validity of the effectiveness index.

Division L was facing a similar problem but without top-management intervention. Its members believed that their problems were given low priority by others in the agency but that these problems would nonetheless have great impact in the future unless solved. They were subsequently proved right in two instances, but meanwhile top management remained almost totally unresponsive. This lack of responsiveness and direction led members of the division to ask what their mission really was: What did the administrator want? This quandary was reflected in their self-appraisal on fulfilling objectives; from subsequent interviews with people in the division we learned that they had checked the lower responses as substitutes for a missing option: "I don't know what the objectives are." Outside rankers took the same dim view of Division L's effectiveness for two major reasons: They thought that members of the division worked with inconsequential problems, and they considered the division director a very difficult person to work with.

The effectiveness rankings by outsiders shown in Table A-5 were unrelated to the self-appraisals. Three divisions, B, E, and L, contributed two-thirds of the variation. We have already discussed that Division B was similar to Division C in NASA. Although many aspects of its work were secret, it was able to cooperate with other units, so that they considered it effective. But within the division there were abundant problems, mostly of a supervisory nature. Although adequate results were produced, the members thought that they could have been much better. Finally, in Division E we found a very important limitation to the self-appraisal approach. The members of this division considered themselves quite effective (3.98), but outsiders ranked them as the least effective division in the agency. This division was composed of highly trained professionals but professionals who had been trained a generation earlier. They used professional standards in making their judgments, but they were outmoded standards. Outside rankers judged these professionals according to more current standards. The self-evaluation approach assumes that respondents will use viable professional standards. If they do not, the validity of the results is questionable.

MEASURING ORGANIZATIONAL EFFECTIVENESS: A SUMMARY

In the ten-hospital and NASA studies we were fortunate enough to find forces operating to keep various professional standards up to date. Hospitals are veritable centers of diffusion for new medical knowledge and techniques. In NASA an aggressive management did all that it could to keep its professional groups apprised of modern advances, and it judged the efforts of these groups against such standards on an almost daily basis. In Alpha Agency top management was more inclined simply to wash its hands of stagnating groups and even to shunt them off to outlying buildings where they would not intrude themselves on the effective work of the agency. It lacked effective internal management partly because of heavy demands made on its leaders to work with other organizations.

We conclude that the effectiveness index is a valid and inexpensive measure except when responses reflect outmoded standards. Such situations can usually be revealed by comparing internal assessments with those of top management and other outside rankers and by examining disagreements through follow-up interviews. The assessments of management were, however, generally less useful than are self-appraisals because managers tended to be oriented toward results. Unless they were given the same criteria as were the self-assessors and often even when they were, their judgments were based almost exclusively on output characteristics. Other outside rankers also gave great weight to output characteristics because that was what was important to them. If the work of the rated divisions was somewhat secret, these rankers were doubly handicapped. We strongly suspect that their judgments were heavily colored by the reputations of other divisions, though we do not have data to prove it. It seems important, therefore, to obtain measures of unit effectiveness from several sources, in order to ensure a clear estimate of the validity of the self-appraisal measure.

B
Correlations of Effectiveness Items

TABLE B-1 Correlations of Effectiveness Items, NASA-2

	PRODUCTIVITY						ADAPTABILITY			
	PRODUC-TIVITY	ADAPT-ABILITY	FLEXI-BILITY	QUAN-TITY	QUAL-ITY	EFFI-CIENCY	ANTICI-PATING PROBLEMS	KEEPING UP TO DATE	PROMPT-NESS OF ADJUST-MENT	PREVA-LENCE OF ADJUST-MENT
Overall effectiveness	.79*	.89	.65	.70	.68	.74	.71	.68	.74	.74
Productivity		.68	.53	.87	.81	.88	.57	.52	.55	.49
Adaptability			.55	.54	.60	.61	.77	.76	.81	.81
Flexibility				.43	.49	.47	.45	.35	.43	.49
Productivity										
Quantity					.53	.67	.45	.39	.45	.39
Quality						.60	.50	.48	.47	.47
Efficiency							.54	.47	.51	.40
Adaptability										
Anticipating problems								.54	.46	.42
Keeping up to date									.43	.43
Promptness of adjustment										.66

*Pearson product-moment correlation coefficients. A missing-data program was used; N = 400-439. Correlations between index items and the indexes of which they are part are indicated by enclosures.

TABLE B-2 Correlations of Effectiveness Items, Alpha Agency

	PRODUCTIVITY						ADAPTABILITY			
	PRODUC-TIVITY	ADAPT-ABILITY	FLEXI-BILITY	QUAN-TITY	QUAL-ITY	EFFI-CIENCY	ANTICI-PATING PROBLEMS	KEEPING UP TO DATE	PROMPT-NESS OF ADJUST-MENT	PREVA-LENCE OF ADJUST-MENT
Overall effectiveness	.64*	.81	.57	.51	.56	.53	.54	.64	.61	.57
Productivity		.55	.31	.79	.79	.81	.44	.44	.35	.31
Adaptability			.43	.38	.49	.44	.61	.73	.80	.74
Flexibility				.20	.30	.23	.15	.36	.56	.37
Productivity										
Quantity					.46	.48	.31	.32	.22	.20
Quality						.41	.40	.38	.34	.40
Efficiency							.37	.36	.27	.36
Adaptability										
Anticipating problems								.31	.22	.31
Keeping up to date									.50	.27
Promptness of adjustment										.32

*Pearson product-moment correlation coefficients. A missing-data program was used. N = 400-439. Correlations between index items and the indexes of which they are part are indicated by enclosures.

TABLE B-3 Correlations of Effectiveness Items, Byberry-1

	PRODUCTIVITY	ADAPTABILITY	FLEXIBILITY	PRODUCTIVITY			ADAPTABILITY			
				QUANTITY	QUALITY	EFFICIENCY	ANTICIPATING PROBLEMS	KEEPING UP TO DATE	PROMPTNESS OF ADJUSTMENT	PREVALENCE OF ADJUSTMENT
Overall effectiveness	.80*	.93	.68	.62	.71	.71	.72	.71	.69	.67
Productivity		.56	.56	.83	.87	.86	.42	.43	.41	.40
Adaptability			.49	.42	.50	.50	.77	.76	.77	.70
Flexibility				.35	.48	.58	.42	.34	.26	.34
Productivity										
Quantity					.63	.54	.33	.30	.29	.26
Quality						.61	.42	.42	.36	.36
Efficiency							.32	.36	.38	.38
Adaptability										
Anticipating problems								.50	.48	.35
Keeping up to date									.48	.48
Promptness of adjustment										.46

*Pearson product-moment correlation coefficients. A missing-data program was used. N = 171-178. Correlations between index items and the indexes of which they are part are indicated by enclosures. Only responses from administrative personnel and those directly involved in the care of patients were included in these data.

TABLE B-4 Correlations of Effectiveness Items, U.S. State Department

	QUALITY	EFFICIENCY	PROMPTNESS OF ADJUSTMENT	SUMMARY OF EFFECTIVENESS*
Productivity				
Quantity	.48†	.57	.39	.51
Quality		.52	.43	.51
Efficiency			.42	.55
Adaptability				
Promptness of adjustment				.49

*No index of effectiveness was constructed because half the appropriate items were not included in this study. For purposes of comparison this single summary item was included: "Overall how would you rate your division or program on effectiveness? How well does it do at fulfilling its mission or achieving its goals?"

†Pearson product-moment correlation coefficients were used; $N > 550$.

C
Key
Questionnaire
Items

The items listed here from the NASA studies were included in all the major studies reported in this volume, though with some slight variations in wording.

EFFECTIVENESS ITEMS

Every worker produces something in his work. It may be a "product" or a "service." But sometimes it is very difficult to identify the product or service. Below are listed some of the products and services being produced in the Office of Administration.

Typed pages
Delivered mail
Dispatched automobiles
Staff papers and studies
Coding systems

Recommended policies and
   procedures
New programs
Classified jobs
Supplying new equipment
Contracts

These are just a few of the things being produced.

We would like you to think carefully of the things that you produce in your work and of the things produced by those people who work around you in your division.

Thinking now of the various things produced by the people you know *in your division*, how much are they producing? CHECK ONE:

_____ (1) Their production is very high
_____ (2) It is fairly high
_____ (3) It is neither high nor low
_____ (4) It is fairly low
_____ (5) It is very low

How good would you say is the *quality* of the products or
services produced by the people you know *in your division?*
CHECK ONE:

_____ (1) Their products or services are of excellent quality
_____ (2) Good quality
_____ (3) Fair quality
_____ (4) Their quality is not too good
_____ (5) Their quality is poor

Do the people in your division seem to get maximum output
from the resources (money, people, equipment, etc.) they have
available? That is, how *efficiently* do they do their work?
CHECK ONE:

_____ (1) They do not work efficiently at all
_____ (2) Not too efficient
_____ (3) Fairly efficient
_____ (4) They are very efficient
_____ (5) They are extremely efficient

How good a job is done by the people in your division in *anticipating* problems that may come up in the future and preventing them from occurring or minimizing their effects?
CHECK ONE:

_____ (1) They do an excellent job in anticipating problems
_____ (2) They do a very good job
_____ (3) A fair job
_____ (4) Not too good a job
_____ (5) They do a poor job in anticipating problems

From time to time newer ways are discovered to organize
work, and newer equipment and techniques are found with
which to do the work. How good a job do the people in your
division do at keeping up with these changes that could affect
the way they do their work? CHECK ONE:

_____ (1) They do a poor job of keeping up to date
_____ (2) Not too good a job
_____ (3) A fair job
_____ (4) They do a good job
_____ (5) They do an excellent job of keeping up to date

When changes are made in the routines or equipment, how *quickly* do the people in your division accept and adjust to these changes? CHECK ONE:

____ (1) Most people accept and adjust to them immediately
____ (2) They adjust very rapidly, but not immediately
____ (3) Fairly rapidly
____ (4) Rather slowly
____ (5) Most people accept and adjust to them very slowly

What *proportion* of the people in your division readily accept and adjust to these changes? CHECK ONE:

____ (1) Considerably less than half of the people accept and adjust to these changes readily
____ (2) Slightly less than half do
____ (3) The majority do
____ (4) Considerably more than half do
____ (5) Practically everyone accepts and adjusts to these changes readily

From time to time emergencies arise, such as crash programs, schedules moved ahead, or a breakdown in the flow of work occurs. When these emergencies occur, they cause work overloads for many people. Some work groups cope with these emergencies more readily and successfully than others. How good a job do the people in your division do at coping with these situations? CHECK ONE:

____ (1) They do a poor job of handling emergency situations
____ (2) They do not do very well
____ (3) They do a fair job
____ (4) They do a good job
____ (5) They do an excellent job of handling these situations

NEGOTIATED-ORDER ITEMS

To what extent do the people you work with *in your division* make an effort to avoid creating problems or interference with each other's duties and responsibilities? CHECK ONE:

____ (1) They try to avoid interfering with each other to a very great extent
____ (2) To a great extent
____ (3) To a fair extent
____ (4) To a small extent

_____ (5) They try to avoid interfering with each other to a very small extent

From time to time problems of coordinating the work of people who must work together arise. When they arise *in your division,* how well are these problems handled? CHECK ONE:

_____ (1) These problems are extremely well handled
_____ (2) Very well handled
_____ (3) Fairly well handled
_____ (4) Not very well handled
_____ (5) They are not handled well at all

To what extent do the people within your division exchange helpful information and ideas? CHECK ONE:

_____ (1) We exchange helpful ideas and information to a great extent
_____ (2) A considerable extent
_____ (3) A fair extent
_____ (4) A small extent
_____ (5) We do not exchange helpful ideas and information at all

COORDINATION ITEMS

How well planned are the work assignments of the people you have to work with *in your division?* CHECK ONE:

_____ (1) The work assignments are extremely well planned
_____ (2) Very well planned
_____ (3) Fairly well planned
_____ (4) Not so well planned
_____ (5) The work assignments are not at all well planned

How well are the different jobs and work activities *in your division* geared together in the direction of meeting the objectives of the division? CHECK ONE:

_____ (1) The jobs and activities are not at all well geared together
_____ (2) Not so well
_____ (3) Fairly well
_____ (4) Very well
_____ (5) The jobs and activities are geared together almost perfectly

RATIONAL-TRUST ITEMS

How closely do the people in the Front Office of the OA[1] follow the policies they establish that affect your work as well as theirs? CHECK ONE:

_____ (1) They follow their own policies extremely closely
_____ (2) They follow them very closely
_____ (3) They follow them fairly closely
_____ (4) They don't follow them too closely
_____ (5) They don't follow them at all
_____ (8) I don't know

How well do the people in the Front Office of the OA understand your needs and problems in your work? CHECK ONE:

_____ (1) They understand my needs and problems perfectly
_____ (2) They understand them very well
_____ (3) Fairly well
_____ (4) Not too well
_____ (5) They don't understand my needs and problems well at all
_____ (8) I don't know

To what extent are the people in the Front Office of the OA fair and reasonable in their decisions that affect your work, *regardless of whether those decisions are favorable to you or not?* CHECK ONE:

_____ (1) They are extremely fair and reasonable
_____ (2) They are very fair and reasonable
_____ (3) They are somewhat fair and reasonable
_____ (4) They are not too fair and reasonable
_____ (5) They are not at all fair and reasonable
_____ (8) I don't know

SUPERVISION ITEMS

How much does your supervisor know about doing each of the jobs in your area? CHECK ONE:

_____ (1) He knows a very great deal about doing the jobs in my area
_____ (2) A great deal

[1]The Office of Administration.

_____ (3) Quite a bit
_____ (4) Some
_____ (5) He knows very little about doing the jobs in my
        area

How well does your supervisor handle the *technical side* of
his job—for example, general expertness, knowledge of job,
technical skills needed, etc.? CHECK ONE:

_____ (1) He handles the technical side of his job extremely
        well
_____ (2) Very well
_____ (3) Fairly well
_____ (4) Not so well
_____ (5) He does not handle the technical side of his job
        at all well

How much help do you feel you get from your supervisor
when you really need it? CHECK ONE:

_____ (1) He never gives me any help when I really need it
_____ (2) Hardly ever gives me any help
_____ (3) Sometimes gives me help
_____ (4) Usually gives me help
_____ (5) He always gives me help when I really need it

Do you feel that your supervisor will go to bat or stand up
for you? CHECK ONE:

_____ (1) No, he won't go to bat for me
_____ (2) Probably won't
_____ (3) May or may not
_____ (4) Probably will
_____ (5) Yes, definitely he will go to bat for me

How free do you feel to discuss important things about your
job with your supervisor? CHECK ONE:

_____ (1) I feel completely free to discuss things about my
        job with my supervisor
_____ (2) Rather free
_____ (3) Fairly free
_____ (4) Not very free
_____ (5) I feel not at all free to discuss things about my job
        with my supervisor

In solving job problems, does your supervisor generally try to get your ideas and opinions? CHECK ONE:

_____ (1) He seldom gets my ideas and opinions in solving job problems
_____ (2) He sometimes does this
_____ (3) He often does this
_____ (4) He almost always does this
_____ (5) He always gets my ideas and opinions in solving job problems

To what extent do you feel that you, personally, can influence the activities and decisions of your supervisor on matters that are of concern to you? CHECK ONE:

_____ (1) I can influence him to a great extent
_____ (2) To a considerable extent
_____ (3) To a moderate extent
_____ (4) To some extent
_____ (5) I can't influence him at all

How well does your supervisor handle the *human relations side* of his job—for example, getting people to work well together, getting individuals to do the best they can, giving recognition for good work done, letting people know where they stand, etc.? CHECK ONE:

_____ (1) He handles the human relations side of his job extremely well
_____ (2) Very well
_____ (3) Fairly well
_____ (4) Not so well
_____ (5) He does not handle the human relations side of his job at all well

How frequently is work time lost because your supervisor fails to do the proper planning and scheduling? CHECK ONE:

_____ (1) Work time is quite frequently lost through his poor planning and scheduling
_____ (2) Frequently
_____ (3) Occasionally
_____ (4) Almost never
_____ (5) Work time is never lost through his poor planning and scheduling

In carrying out the basic tasks of your job, does your supervisor supervise you closely or does he put you on your own? CHECK ONE:

_____ (1) He uses very general supervision; I am definitely on my own

_____ (2) He uses fairly general supervision; I am pretty much on my own

_____ (3) He uses a moderate amount of supervision

_____ (4) He uses fairly close supervision

_____ (5) He uses very close supervision; he doesn't put me on my own

How well do you feel you understand the work problems and needs that your supervisor has? CHECK ONE:

_____ (1) I have complete understanding of his work problems and needs

_____ (2) Considerable understanding

_____ (3) Some understanding

_____ (4) A little understanding

_____ (5) I have no understanding of his work problems and needs

How well do you feel your supervisor understands the work problems and needs which you have? CHECK ONE:

_____ (1) He has complete understanding of my work problems and needs

_____ (2) Considerable understanding

_____ (3) Some understanding

_____ (4) A little understanding

_____ (5) He has no understanding of my work problems and needs

How well does your supervisor handle the *administrative side* of his job—for example, planning and scheduling the work, indicating clearly when work is to be finished, assigning the right job to the right man, inspecting and following up on the work that is done, etc.? CHECK ONE:

_____ (1) He does not handle the administrative side of his job at all well

_____ (2) Not so well

_____ (3) Fairly well
_____ (4) Very well
_____ (5) He handles the administrative side of his job extremely well

How well does your supervisor understand the "big picture" of what NASA is all about—does he see how NASA's mission relates to the social, economic, and political environment of the country? CHECK ONE:

_____ (1) He understands the "big picture" extremely well
_____ (2) Very well
_____ (3) Fairly well
_____ (4) Not so well
_____ (5) He does not understand the "big picture" at all well
_____ (8) I don't know

How good a job does your supervisor do at personally representing your work group in dealings with other groups in NASA or outside organizations? CHECK ONE:

_____ (1) He does a rather poor job at representing us
_____ (2) Fair job
_____ (3) Good job
_____ (4) Very good job
_____ (5) He does an excellent job at representing us

To the best of your knowledge, is your supervisor a better *subordinate with his supervisor* than he is a *supervisor over his subordinates?* CHECK ONE:

_____ (1) He is a much better subordinate than he is a supervisor
_____ (2) Better subordinate than supervisor
_____ (3) He is equally good as a subordinate and as a supervisor
_____ (4) Better supervisor than subordinate
_____ (5) He is a much better supervisor than he is a subordinate

How well does your supervisor handle the *institutional leadership side* of his job—for example, creating and formulating policy; handling matters of the agency's relationships to outside organizations, agencies, and groups; understanding the importance and relationships of the agency's mission on the political, social, and economic environment? CHECK ONE:

_____ (1) He handles the institutional leadership side of his job extremely well
_____ (2) Very well
_____ (3) Fairly well
_____ (4) Not so well
_____ (5) He does not handle the institutional leadership side of his job at all well
_____ (8) I don't know

How often does your supervisor belittle you, or act sarcastic toward you? CHECK ONE:

_____ (1) He very frequently belittles me
_____ (2) Frequently
_____ (3) Occasionally
_____ (4) Seldom
_____ (5) He never belittles me

IF YOU CHECKED "He never belittles me" IN THE QUESTION ABOVE SKIP THE NEXT TWO ITEMS BELOW AND GO ON...

After your supervisor has belittled you or been sarcastic in his criticism of your work, how much trouble do you have getting back to work? CHECK ONE:

_____ (1) I have a great deal of trouble getting back to work
_____ (2) Considerable trouble
_____ (3) A fair amount of trouble
_____ (4) Very little trouble
_____ (5) I have no trouble at all getting back to work

After your supervisor has been sarcastic or belittling about your work, do you take it out on other people, either at work or at home? CHECK ONE:

_____ (1) I very often take it out on other people
_____ (2) Often
_____ (3) Occasionally
_____ (4) Seldom
_____ (5) I never take it out on other people

How often do you become irritated or annoyed with your supervisor? CHECK ONE:

_____ (1) I am very often annoyed with my supervisor
_____ (2) Often
_____ (3) Occasionally
_____ (4) Seldom
_____ (5) I never become irritated or annoyed with my super-
      visor

How much confidence and trust do you have in your super-visor? CHECK ONE:

_____ (1) I have no confidence and trust in my supervisor at all
_____ (2) Not very much confidence and trust
_____ (3) A fair amount
_____ (4) A great deal
_____ (5) I have complete confidence and trust in my super-
      visor

How much confidence and trust does your supervisor have in you? CHECK ONE:

_____ (1) He has no confidence and trust in me at all
_____ (2) Not very much
_____ (3) A fair amount
_____ (4) A great deal
_____ (5) My supervisor has complete confidence and trust
      in me
_____ (8) I don't know

Some people can be described as "approachable" (easy to talk with), while others are "distant" (not easy to talk with). Would you describe your supervisor as "approachable" or "distant"? CHECK ONE:

_____ (1) My supervisor is very definitely approachable
_____ (2) More approachable than distant
_____ (3) Approachable on some things, distant on others
_____ (4) More distant than approachable
_____ (5) My supervisor is very definitely distant

To what extent are decisions in your division made by groups, that is, by a supervisor and his subordinates working through a matter together and agreeing on what should be done? CHECK ONE:

____ (1) Such group decision making is never done in my division
____ (2) It is rarely done
____ (3) Sometimes done
____ (4) Fairly often done
____ (5) Such group decision making is done very frequently in my division

Does your supervisor deal with his subordinates on a man-to-man basis, or does he deal with them primarily as a group? CHECK ONE:

____ (1) He uses group methods of supervision entirely
____ (2) He uses group methods more than man-to-man methods
____ (3) He uses group and man-to-man methods about equally
____ (4) He uses man-to-man methods more than group methods
____ (5) He uses man-to-man methods of supervision entirely

All in all, how effective a job do you think your supervisor is doing? CHECK ONE:

____ (1) He is doing a rather poor job
____ (2) A fair job
____ (3) A good job
____ (4) A very good job
____ (5) He is doing an excellent job

Index

72 73 74 75 7 6 5 4 3 2 1